# Maximizing Mental Health Services
## Proven Practices that Promote Emotional Well-Being

Nicholas D. Young

Melissa A. Mumby

Jennifer A. Smolinski

Cognitive Science and Psychology

VERNON PRESS

Copyright © 2020 Vernon Press, an imprint of Vernon Art and Science Inc, on behalf of the author.

All rights reserved. No part of this publication may be reproduced, stored in a retrieval system, or transmitted in any form or by any means, electronic, mechanical, photocopying, recording, or otherwise, without the prior permission of Vernon Art and Science Inc.

www.vernonpress.com

*In the Americas:*
Vernon Press
1000 N West Street,
Suite 1200, Wilmington,
Delaware 19801
United States

*In the rest of the world:*
Vernon Press
C/Sancti Espiritu 17,
Malaga, 29006
Spain

Cognitive Science and Psychology

Library of Congress Control Number: 2019943250

ISBN: 978-1-62273-840-3

Also available:

978-1-62273-767-3 [Hardback]; 978-1-62273-791-8 [PDF, E-Book]

Product and company names mentioned in this work are the trademarks of their respective owners. While every care has been taken in preparing this work, neither the authors nor Vernon Art and Science Inc. may be held responsible for any loss or damage caused or alleged to be caused directly or indirectly by the information contained in it.

Every effort has been made to trace all copyright holders, but if any have been inadvertently overlooked the publisher will be pleased to include any necessary credits in any subsequent reprint or edition.

Cover design by Vernon Press using elements designed by Freepik.

# Table of Contents

**Acknowledgement** — v

**Foreword** — vii

**Preface** — xi

Chapter One
**The Mental Health Epidemic: An Introduction** — 1

Chapter Two
**In Pursuit of Improved Therapeutic Outcomes:
Understanding the Potency of Evidence-Based Practices** — 13

Chapter Three
**Promoting Positive Change One Client at a Time:
Evidenced-Based Individual Therapy Practices** — 23

Chapter Four
**Engaging the Clan:
Evidenced-Based Family Therapy Practices** — 37

Chapter Five
**Expanding the Support System:
Evidenced-Based Group Therapy Practices** — 49

Chapter Six
**When it Takes Two to Make a Personal Life Work:
Evidenced-Based Couples Therapy Practices** — 61

Chapter Seven
**Respecting Individual Differences:
Strategies for Working with Special Populations** — 75

Chapter Eight
**Understanding the Value of the Therapist: Change Agent
Characteristics that Promote Positive Outcomes**     89

Chapter Nine
**Contemporary Therapeutic Approaches:
Cutting-Edge Practices with Promise**     97

Chapter Ten
**Professional Resources for Counselors:
Organizations and EBP Resources**     109

**Acronyms**     119

**References**     121

**About the Authors**     137

# Acknowledgement

We wish to thank Sue Clark for once again lending us her expertise by professionally editing this book. Without her eagle eye and careful attention to writing conventions, we would not have been able to balance the words, intent and meaning in this manuscript as carefully as we did. We appreciate not only her editing acumen, but also her friendship. Thank you, Sue, for being who you are and supporting our efforts at every turn. We are all better off for having you in our lives.

# Foreword

Over the last decade, the integration of behavioral health services into primary care centers has become increasingly more common. Due to a lack of access to behavioral treatment, approximately 70% of patients with a behavioral health problem initially present their problem to a primary care provider (PCP) prior to seeking formal treatment (Cunningham, 2009). Furthermore, 30% to 50% of patients in the primary care setting have a behavioral health diagnosis (Cunningham, 2009). The result of such a disclosure by a patient often leads to a referral to a behavioral health specialist outside the primary care clinic; however, only 10% of patients will follow through with the referral (Cunningham, 2009). Convenience is key as patients are more likely to elect to see the behavioral health specialist if the individual is within the same practice as the PCP (Johnson, 2017).

The health-care delivery system has evolved, and both medicine and psychology are no longer operating in different silos as they once did (Johnson, 2017). Recognizing that the majority of those suffering from behavioral health disorders first acknowledge an issue to the primary care doctor, the National Health Reform Act of 2010 emphasized the need for behavioral care providers (BCP) to be present within the primary care center (Oberlander, 2010).

The BCP not only functions as a primary care psychotherapist but also educates physicians, physician assistants, and nurse practitioners on the need and use of various behavioral interventions to help facilitate positive behavioral change. The importance of the BCP to understand and utilize evidence-based practices (EBPs) in psychotherapy is, therefore, paramount as these providers have a substantial responsibility to utilize efficacious psychotherapeutic interventions.

The use of a physician assistant as a behavioral medicine provider is a cost-effective way to increase access to prescriptive psychotherapeutic services. With the development of post-graduate residencies that train these providers, physician assistants can gain advanced training in psychopharmacology, behavioral interventions, and evidence-based practices in psychotherapy (PhysicianAssistantEDU, 2019).

With the rise of prescriptive psychotropic medications to immediately treat behavioral health conditions, the undesired side effects such as gastrointestinal issues, weight gain, and loss of sex drive to serious side effects such as metabolic syndrome and cardiac abnormalities carry a heavy burden for both prescribers and patients. Within the Hippocratic Oath, one of the promises medical providers take as they begin their journey in medicine is "first, do no harm" (or "primum non nocere," the Latin translation from the original Greek). There is a feeling amongst providers, however, that they are winning the battle, i.e., mental health symptomatology, yet losing the war, i.e., the patient's overall health.

Restoring psychotherapy as a first-line intervention is perhaps the greatest asset for both the patient and treating provider. It is vital, however, that the psychotherapeutic interventions utilized by the treating provider must be based on scientifically supported evidence as the patient deserves relief from their symptomatology with the least amount of intrusion, without harm, within the shortest amount of time.

In *Maximizing Mental Health Services: Proven Practices that Promote Emotional Well-Being*, the authors skillfully outline evidence-based therapeutic practices for individual therapy, family therapy, and group therapy that promote improved therapeutic outcomes. This is a great resource for students entering the healthcare arena, the individual psychotherapist in private practice, the behavioral care provider in a busy primary care center, as well as primary care providers themselves and the everyday person interested in their own behavioral health.

Stephen Lee, DBH, MS, PA-C
Assistant Professor, Physician Assistant Program
Westfield State University, Westfield, MA

**About Dr. Lee:**

Dr. Stephen Lee earned a Doctor of Behavioral Health and is a clinical professor in Westfield State University's Physician Assistant Program. He has taught behavioral medicine at various graduate programs including Springfield College, Bay Path University, Cummings Graduate Institute for Behavioral Health Studies, and Quinnipiac University. Dr. Lee has over 25 years of experience in medicine, including over a decade in military medicine practicing as a Navy Corpsman and an Army Battalion Medical Officer for a mountain infantry unit. He is the founder of a behavioral health practice, *Synergistic Health Services*, in Connecticut that provides psychotherapy and medication management services as well as consults with medical practices around the country to integrate behavioral health services into their primary care clinics. He has piloted an integrated behavioral health practice into two large primary care centers in Connecticut and has partnered with several health care systems to create a Post-Graduate Integrated Behavioral Health Residency Program to increase access to behavioral health services in underserved areas. He was selected by the International Federation of Green Crescents to serve as an expert in addiction medicine and represent the United States for a conference consisting of a coalition of 52 countries to address and combat addiction around the world.

# Preface

In an ever-changing and at times unpredictable world, the concept of what constitutes emotional well-being and appropriate mental health can seem difficult to grasp and even more difficult to embrace. *Maximizing Mental Health Services: Proven Practices that Promote Emotional Well-Being* was written for mental health professionals, professors, graduate students, as well as individuals and family members who are interested in learning more about therapeutic practices and their effect on well-being. This tome will be helpful to all those who are struggling with personal issues and who need to infuse positivity, safety, and resolution into their lives with the help of a trained professional. The path involved in moving from mental illness and distress to mental health and wellness takes time, a commitment to ethical practices, and a deep understanding of the multitude of evidence-based practices that are available to therapists and counselors to use.

Our desire to write this book arose from the following concerns:

- *Our understanding that an estimated 44 million people will be diagnosed with a mental illness in 2019 alone and these individuals deserve appropriate care;*
- *Our knowledge that positive mental health is essential to living a life that is replete with fulfilling emotions, experiences, and friendships and that these are within everyone's reach;*
- *Our desire to ensure that the next generation has access to quality mental health care that is specific to their needs, which is offered by practitioners who are well versed in how to identify and treat individuals, families, couples, and groups appropriately;*
- *Our awareness that mental health professionals perform a much-needed task and without a clear and deep understanding of evidence-based practices, they may not be able to fully help their clients;*

- *Our belief that in sharing the latest in evidence-based practices, those seeking emotional well-being will find ways to cope and conquer whatever is holding them back from creating their best version of themselves.*

With those in need of mental health services climbing into the millions, more than ever before practitioners need to have a clear understanding of therapies that can help their clients become whole again. In the chapters to follow, the authors take time to help the reader understand the nuances of mental health and mental illness and how it manifests itself in a variety of ways in different populations. They then offer a clear explanation of evidence-based practices and how they can be used to help individuals, couples, families, and groups to understand, cope with, and, when possible, overcome the issues that exist in their lives. In order to provide as much support to the reader as possible, there is a chapter on promising practices and a resource chapter to help in accessing more information included as well.

This book was written by a highly seasoned team of practitioners and scholars including, but not limited to, a psychologist, a counselor, and an educator with a wealth of experience working with individuals who suffer from mental illness. It seeks to add to the body of literature that captures pertinent information on the mental health illness while emphasizing evidenced-based and related practices that hold promise in addressing it.

*Maximizing Mental Health Services: Proven Practices that Promote Emotional Well-Being* places a premium on supporting the therapist and client in meaningful ways. With so much at stake, it has become increasingly more important to find avenues for mental well-being to be cultivated and nurtured so that all human beings can be emotionally strong and vital members of their families and communities. The authors hope that this book is a building block towards a new beginning for those who need it, regardless if that is the professor or student, therapist, the client, or the family of a loved one in need.

# Chapter One

# The Mental Health Epidemic: An Introduction

Mental health is an integral and essential component of a person's overall health and well-being that includes aspects of physical, mental and social well-being and not merely the absence of disease and/or mental disorders or disabilities (Centers for Disease Control and Prevention, 2018; Office of Juvenile Justice and Delinquency Prevention, 2017; World Health Organization, 2018). Mental well-being is comprised of an individual's ability to recognize their individual capabilities and the ability to cope with normal life stress, work productively, and make contributions to society (Centers for Disease Control and Prevention, 2018; Office of Juvenile Justice and Delinquency Prevention, 2017; World Health Organization, 2018).

Mental health is essential to the collective and individual ability to think, emote, interact, work, and simply enjoy life and as such, there are multiple social, psychological, and biological factors that will determine an individual's level of mental health at any given time (World Health Organization, 2018; Centers for Disease Control and Prevention, 2018). People exposed to recognized risk factors such as violence and persistent socio-economic pressures are more likely to have a poor state of mental health than those individuals who are not exposed to those risk factors. Poor mental health is also linked to rapid social change, stressful work conditions, gender discrimination, social exclusion, an unhealthy lifestyle, physical ill-health and human rights violations (World Health Organization, 2018).

## Mental Health versus Mental Illness

It is important to note that, although the terms are frequently used interchangeably, poor mental health and mental illness are very different. Individuals can experience poor mental health and not be diagnosed with a mental illness and, likewise, a person can be diagnosed with a mental illness yet experience periods of physical, mental, and social well-being (Centers for Disease Control and Prevention, 2018).

Mental illness is made up of a variety of acute or chronic conditions that affect how a person thinks or feels, that may change mood or behavior (such as depression, anxiety, bipolar disorder, or schizophrenia), as well as an individual's ability to relate to others and adequately perform life's daily functions (Centers for Disease Control and Prevention, 2018). There is no known single cause of mental illness and it is the most common health condition in the United States (Centers for Disease Control and Prevention, 2018).

Research has demonstrated that more than 50% of the population will be diagnosed with a mental illness or disorder at some point in their lifetime and that one in five Americans, an estimated 44 million adults, will experience a mental illness in any given year (Centers for Disease Control and Prevention, 2018; Edwards-Tate, 2018; Mental Health America, 2018b; National Alliance on Mental Health, 2019b; Tucci & Moukaddam, 2017). It is also important to note that 1 in 25 Americans, or an estimated 9.8 million adults, lives with a serious mental illness, such as schizophrenia, bipolar disorder, or major depression (Centers for Disease Control and Prevention, 2018; Edwards-Tate, 2018; Mental Health America, 2018b; National Alliance on Mental Health, 2019b; Tucci & Moukaddam, 2017).

Although these rates are staggering, the states of Massachusetts, Vermont, Maine, Minnesota, North Dakota, and Delaware have the lowest incidences of mental illness in the country (Edwards-Tate, 2018). This may be attributed to the fact that these states have the best access to insurance and responsive mental health treatment programs (Edwards-Tate, 2018).

There are numerous factors that contribute to an individual's risk for mental illness. Early adverse life experiences, including trauma and/or abuse, such as child abuse, sexual assault, or witnessing violence, as well as an individual's experiences in relation to additional chronic medical conditions, such as cancer, place an individual at higher risk for mental illness (Centers for Disease Control and Prevention, 2018). Biological factors, such as genes or chemical imbalances in the brain, the use of alcohol or recreational drugs, and simply having the feeling of loneliness or isolation, play an integral part in mental illness (Centers for Disease Control and Prevention, 2018).

## Increasing Rates of Mental Health Disorders Worldwide

There are numerous mental disorders that all present differently; yet, they can be characterized by a combination of abnormal thoughts, perceptions, emotions, and behaviors (World Health Organization, 2018). Mental disorders affect individuals worldwide and an estimated 15-20% (1 in 6 people) of the world's population suffer from one or more mental or substance use disorder (Ritchie & Roser, 2018). More specifically, approximately 1.1 billion individuals worldwide had a mental or substance abuse disorder in 2016; 4% of the world's population was diagnosed with anxiety, 300 million individuals were diagnosed with depression, 60 million were diagnosed with bipolar, 23 million were diagnosed with schizophrenia, and 50 million were diagnosed with dementia (Ritchie & Roser, 2018; Tucci & Moukaddam, 2017; World Health Organization, 2018).

Mental and substance use disorders account for approximately 7% of the global disease burden, with specific countries having individual rates as high as 13-14% (Ritchie & Roser, 2018). Although these numbers may be staggering, research demonstrates that mental illness statistics are significantly underreported worldwide, particularly at lower income levels where data is scarce and there is less attention to and treatment for mental health disorders (Ritchie & Roser, 2018).

Mood disorders, such as major depression, dysthymic disorder, and bipolar disorder, are the third most common cause of hospitalization in the United States for those aged 18 to 44 (National Alliance on Mental Health, 2019b; World Health Organization, 2018). It is anticipated that by 2030, depression will be the number one cause of disease worldwide (Tucci & Moukaddam, 2017). There are currently an estimated 60 million people across the globe who suffer from depression and an estimated 21 million who suffer from schizophrenia (Ritchie & Roser, 2018; Tucci & Moukaddam, 2017).

**Depression.** All forms of depressive disorders can experience a host of issues to include reduced concentration, attention, self-esteem, and/or self-confidence, ideals of guilt, unworthiness, self-harm, and/or suicide, pessimistic views of the future, disturbed sleep, and diminished appetite (Ritchie & Roser, 2018). Across the globe, individuals with these symptoms of depression range between 2% and 6%, with older individuals (70 + years) having the highest risk (Ritchie & Roser, 2018).

In 2016, an estimated 268 million people worldwide experienced one or more forms of depression (Ritchie & Roser, 2018). Research conducted in the United States demonstrated that among 41 million insurance carriers, 5.8% were diagnosed with major depression diagnoses compared to 4.6% in 2013 (Fox, 2018).

**Bipolar disorder.** Bipolar is characterized by repeated episodes in which the patient's mood and activity levels are significantly disturbed either through an elevation or lowering of mood, energy, and activity (Ritchie & Roser, 2018). In 2016, there were approximately 40 billion people across the world with bipolar, although the prevalence of bipolar ranged from 0.4% to 1.5% by country (Ritchie & Roser, 2018).

**Anxiety disorders.** Anxiety disorders can occur in a number of forms, such as phobic, social, obsessive-compulsive disorder (OCD), post-traumatic disorder (PTSD), or generalized anxiety disorders. Although each subset has its unique symptoms and diagnostic criteria, collective symptoms include apprehension, motor tension, and autonomic over activity (Ritchie & Roser, 2018). Global prevalence varies from 2.5% to 6.5% by country with an overall estimated 275 million people in 2016 experiencing some form of an anxiety disorder, making anxiety the most predominant mental health or neurodevelopmental disorder (Ritchie & Roser, 2018).

### Mental Health Role in Preventing Suicide

Research has consistently attributed mental health disorders to a significant number of indirect deaths through suicide and self-harm; yet, suicide-related deaths may not always be attributable to mental health disorders (Ritchie & Roser, 2018). In high-income countries, analyses indicate that up to 90% of suicide deaths result from underlying mental and substance use disorders; however, in middle to lower-income countries, this figure is markedly lower (National Alliance for Mental Health, 2019; Ritchie & Roser, 2018).

Across the world, suicide rates have increased over 60% in the last 45 years with the highest rate occurring in Lithuania (Tucci & Moukaddam, 2017). In the United States, the rate of suicide has increased by 24% over a 15 year period and is the tenth leading cause of death in the U.S. and the second leading cause of death among people aged 15-34 (Higgins, 2017; National Alliance on Mental Health, 2019b; Tucci & Moukaddam, 2017; World Health Organization, 2018).

### Mental Health as a Psychical Health Factor

Those individuals living with serious mental illness are also at an increased risk of physical health problems, such as heart disease, diabetes, and HIV and die an average of 25 years earlier, mainly due to treatable medical conditions (Fox, 2018; National Alliance on Mental Health, 2019b; World Health Organization, 2018). As a result, the United States mental health budget has exponentially increased from $33 billion to more than $80 billion over the last 25 years (Adi, Pagel, Whitaker, & Uzbanek, 2019). Furthermore, in the United States, mental illness has become the second most common cause of disability, as evidenced by disability awards from the Social Security Administration (Higgins, 2017).

**Role of Mental Health in Criminal Behavior**

Mental illnesses that go untreated also play a significant role in criminal or homicidal behavior, particularly where substance abuse or unemployment is also prevalent (Edwards-Tate, 2018). The number of people being committed to United States prisons with mental illnesses has significantly increased over the last 65 years. It is estimated that approximately 20% of state prisoners and 24% of local jail prisoners have a recent history of a mental health condition, including psychotic disorders (Edwards-Tate, 2018; National Alliance on Mental Health, 2019a; 2019b).

**Mental Health and the Elderly**

It is estimated that, between 2015 and 2050, the proportion of older adults across the globe will double from 12% to 22%, rising from 900 million to 2 billion people over age 60 (World Health Organization, 2017). While most adults 60 years of age and older make valuable contributions to society and have good mental health, many are at risk of developing mental disorders, neurological disorders or substance use problems as well as other physical health conditions and are more likely to experience several conditions simultaneously (Miller, 2016; World Health Organization, 2017).

More than 20% of older adults suffer from a mental or neurological disorder and 6.6% of all disability is attributed to these types of (Newman, 2017; World Health Organization, 2017; Miller, 2016). The most common mental disorders amongst this age group are depression (7%), dementia (5%), anxiety (3.8%) and substance use (1%), which also accounts for 25% of the deaths from self-harm (Newman, 2017; World Health Organization, 2017). More specifically, 50 million people worldwide live with dementia and the total number of older adults with dementia is projected to increase to 82 million in 2030 and 152 million in 2050 (World Health Organization, 2017). Adults 85 and older have the highest suicide rate of any age group, almost 6 times that of the general population (Miller, 2016; Newman, 2017).

Mental health problems in older adults are on the rise, although they are typically under-identified by health-care professionals and older adults themselves. The world's baby boomers, who carry a higher predisposition to suicide, will account for a doubling of individuals age 65 and over, bringing the number from 46 million to 98 million by 2060 (Miller, 2016; Newman, 2017). At the same time, the number of therapists that work with the elderly is projected to decline, resulting in less than one therapist per 6000 clients who suffer from a mental health disorder or substance use issue (Newman, 2017).

As life stressors increase, such as significant ongoing loss in capabilities, decline in functional ability, bereavement, and decrease in socioeconomic status, they can leave older adults feeling isolated, lonely, and distressed (World Health Organization, 2017). Mental health can also have an impact on physical health and vice versa; for example, older adults with heart disease have higher rates of depression and untreated depression in an older adult with heart disease can adversely affect its outcome (Newman, 2017; World Health Organization, 2017).

Older adults are also more susceptible to elder abuse, including physical, verbal, psychological, abandonment, and neglect. Research suggests that 1 in 6 older people experience elder abuse, which can lead to significant psychological consequences, including depression and anxiety (World Health Organization, 2017).

**Mental Health in Youth and Young Adults**

There are more than 50 million public school students in the U.S. and an estimated 21.4% of youth ages 13-18, and 13% of students ages 8-15, experience a severe mental health disorder (National Alliance on Mental Illness, 2019; Fox, 2018; Anderson & Cardoza, 2016). For those students ages 14-21 receiving special education, 37% have a mental health condition and drop out of school, the highest rate among students of any disability group (National Alliance on Mental Health, 2019a).

According to research completed on 41 million carriers of commercial insurance, the diagnoses of major depression rose by 33% from 2013 to 2016. Specifically, 2.6% of youth ages 12 to 17 were diagnosed with major depression, a 63% increase between 2013 and 2016 and 4.4% of young adults aged 18-34 were diagnosed, an increase of 47% (Fox, 2018). Evidence suggested that this rise in depression may be due to a combination of feeling rushed, pressured, isolated, impaired sleep, and a lack of connectedness, potentially fueled by video games and social media, which can perpetuate isolation and cause poor school performance and impaired sleep (Fox, 2018).

Those children that have a mental health disorder, not just a diagnosis of depression, inexorably miss out on opportunities for learning and building relationships and nearly 80% of those affected by a mental health disorder will not receive counseling, therapy, medication, or any treatment at all (Fox, 2018; Anderson & Cardoza, 2016). Schools are faced with, on average, 21-27 students per class, 491 students per counselor, 1,151students per nurse, and 1,400 students per psychologist, making it extremely difficult to provide students with the services they need (Anderson & Cardoza, 2016).

Research has also demonstrated that there is a developing epidemic of mental health issues in emerging adults, particularly college students (ages 18-24) (Eagan et al., 2016; Henriques, 2014). Evidence suggests that this particular age group has greater levels of stress and psychopathology now than at any other time in history with 34.5% of incoming first-time college students reporting that they habitually felt anxious (Eagan et al., 2016; Henriques, 2014).

Adjusting to the academic demands of college, being away from home (many for the first time), and forming new social groups, are only some of the factors that contribute to students' stress, anxiety, or depression levels, especially among students that have a disability, chronic illness, or psychological disorder (Eagan et al., 2016). For college students that already have a pre-existing stressor, such as a disability or mental health disorder, they are even more likely to feel anxious as compared to their peers (Eagan et al., 2016).

Not only has the rate of anxiety increased among college students, but the rate of depression has also skyrocketed over the last twenty years. College student surveys reveal that approximately 57% of women and 40% of men reported experiencing episodes of overwhelming anxiety and 33% of women and 27% of men reported feeling so depressed it interfered with their ability to function (Henriques, 2014). The increasing rate of depression is concerning as depression is known to be linked to suicide and evidence demonstrates that the suicide rate among young adults ages 15-24 has tripled over the last sixty years and is now the second most common cause of death among college students (Henriques, 2014).

The increase in the number of students affected by mental health problems has also been felt by college counseling centers. Of the college counseling center directors surveyed, 95% believed that the number of students with significant psychological problems is a growing concern and 70% of those directors believed that the number of students with severe psychological problems had increased in the year prior to the study (Henriques, 2014). Students with mental health concerns anticipated making greater use of the counseling services (Eagan et al., 2016).

**Youth in the Juvenile Justice System**

Research has consistently shown that youth in the juvenile justice system have substantially higher rates of behavioral health conditions than those in the general population (Mental Health America, 2018b). In the United States, approximately two million youth become involved in the juvenile justice system each year and of those youth, 70% have at least one mental health condition and at least 20% live with a serious mental illness, a rate that is three times higher than that of the general youth population (Mental Health America, 2018b; National Alliance on Mental Health, 2019a; National Center for Mental Health and Juvenile Justice and National Juvenile Justice Network, 2014; Office of Juvenile Justice and Delinquent Prevention, 2017).

The relationship between mental health issues and involvement in the juvenile justice system is complicated and it is difficult to separate out the correlation and causation, if any, between the two (Office of Juvenile Justice and Delinquency Protection, 2017). Many youths who suffer from various mental health disorders and co-occurring disorders land in the juvenile justice system because they need mental health services and do not have access to them within their community (National Alliance on Mental Health, 2018a; National Center for Mental Health and Juvenile Justice and National Juvenile Justice Network, 2014).

For these youth, mental health disorders and substance use are often overlooked, misdiagnosed, or inadequately addressed by social service agencies and exposure to abuse and exploitation within the juvenile justice system leaves them more likely to experience adverse consequences (National Center for Mental Health and Juvenile Justice and National Juvenile Justice Network, 2014).

There are some youths in the juvenile justice system who do not enter with a mental disorder; yet, certain risk factors can increase the occurrence of both mental health and problem behaviors (Office of Juvenile Justice and Delinquency Prevention, 2017). Exposure to the violence that occurs in juvenile detention facilities can create and/or exacerbate mental health issues such as posttraumatic stress and increase the occurrence of delinquent behavior.

At least 75% of youth in the juvenile justice system have experienced traumatic victimization and 93% have experienced adverse experiences such as child abuse and family violence, putting them at an increased risk for posttraumatic stress syndrome (Mental Health America, 2018a; Office of Juvenile Justice and Delinquency Prevention, 2017). Juvenile detention and correctional facilities can create and/or increase mental health issues due to overcrowding, separation from support systems, and/or solitary confinement (Office of Juvenile Justice and Delinquency Prevention, 2017).

Contributing to the rise of mental health issues, youth in the juvenile justice system do not receive the treatment they need, resulting in youth getting worse and/or developing other mental health issues (National Alliance on Mental Health, 2019a). According to an investigation by the U.S. Department of Justice, mental health services in the juvenile justice system are inadequate, unavailable, or often have barriers to services including insufficient resources, lack of appropriate staffing, and lack of appropriate staff training (National Center for Mental Health and Juvenile Justice and National Juvenile Justice Network, 2014).

Research has demonstrated that of those youth screened and/or assessed in the juvenile justice system, approximately 76% suffered from a substance use disorder, 33% suffered from high anxiety, 14% had attention deficit/hyperactivity disorder (ADHD), 12% had depression, and 12% suffered from posttraumatic stress disorder, while 39% met the threshold for more than one mental health problem (Office of Juvenile Justice and Delinquency Prevention, 2017).

## Connection Between Mental Health Epidemic and Substance Abuse Crisis

Of the 20.2 million adults in the U.S. who suffer from a substance use disorder, research states that 50.5% of them also suffer from a mental illness (Bussing-Birks, 2019; McDonald, 2018; National Alliance on Mental Health, 2019b). In this situation, it is difficult to know which came first, the substance abuse or the mental health disorder (McDonald, 2018; National Institute on Drug Abuse, 2018; Villa, n.d.). What we do know is that those adults living with mental health issues may never seek treatment and instead, turn to substance abuse as a form of self-medication (McDonald, 2018; Villa, n.d.).

Research has shown that individuals with an existing mental illness consume an estimated 38% percent of all alcohol, 44% of all cocaine, and 40% of all cigarettes while those individuals who have experienced a mental illness at any point in the lives, consume an estimated 69% of all the alcohol, 84% of all the cocaine, and 68% of all cigarettes (Bussing-Birks, 2019). For those who do seek treatment, the number of psychiatric drug prescriptions is surging across the globe and these drugs may be contributing to the rise in mental health issues as many of them can worsen or even bring about symptoms of mental illness (Adi et al., 2019; Villa, n.d.).

Another contributing factor to the rise in mental health issues is that drug addiction is classified as a mental illness and as such, the more people that become addicted to drugs, the more people will be considered to have a mental illness (Villa, n.d.). Addiction is a chronic and relapsing disease as it causes distinct brain changes that disrupt a person's hierarchy of needs and makes drug use a priority. Their ability to control the compulsion to use substances is significantly diminished and promotes continued drug use even though the individual knows it is causing harm (Villa, n.d.).

It is well-known that people who struggle with substance abuse and addiction also have co-occurring mental health illness (Bussing-Birks, 2019; Villa, n.d.). Research shows that in 2016, 8.2 million adults had a co-occurring mental illness and substance use disorder, and of those 8.2 million people, only 48.1% received treatment for either their mental health disorder or their addiction (Villa, n.d.). Among those people that suffered from non-alcohol substance use disorders, 28% had co-occurring anxiety disorders, 26% had mood disorders, 18% had antisocial personality disorder, and 7% suffered from schizophrenia (Villa, n.d.).

The comorbidity between mental illness, including drug addiction, and substance abuse disorders may occur via one of three pathways to include (1) common risk factors between both mental illness and substance abuse; (2) mental illness may contribute to substance abuse and addiction; or (3) substance abuse and addiction can contribute to the development of mental illness (National Institute on Drug Abuse, 2018).

**Common Risk Factors for Mental Illness**

Common risk factors include genetic vulnerabilities and environmental factors. It is estimated that 40–60% of an individual's vulnerability to substance use disorders is attributable to genetics (National Institute on Drug Abuse, 2018; Villa, n.d.). Many of the same areas of the brain are affected by both substance abuse disorders and other mental illnesses; for example, the parts of the brain that mediate reward, decision making, and impulse control are all disrupted by both substance abuse disorders and mental illnesses such as schizophrenia and depression (National Institute on Drug Abuse, 2018).

Environmental factors such as trauma, adverse childhood experiences, and chronic stress are also associated with an increased risk of substance use disorders and mental illnesses. Research has repeatedly shown that stress is a risk factor for a variety of mental illnesses and thus provides a neurobiological link between the disease process of substance abuse disorders and mental health disorders (National Institute on Drug Abuse, 2018).

**Mental Illness as a Contributor to Substance Abuse and Vice Versa**

Research has established that there are certain mental ailments that are risk factors in developing a substance use disorder, particularly for those individuals with severe, mild, or even subclinical mental disorders that may use drugs to self-medicate. A person diagnosed with bipolar who chooses to self-medicate with cocaine, for example, may feel a temporary reduction of their symptoms, but prolonged periods of cocaine use will, in reality, worsen the symptoms and even contribute to the progression of the mental illness (National Institute on Drug Abuse, 2018).

Likewise, substance use can lead to changes in the same areas of the brain that are affected by mental disorders. Drug use that precedes the first symptoms of a mental illness may produce changes in the brain structure and function that stimulate an underlying predisposition to develop that mental illness (National Institute on Drug Abuse, 2018).

## Final Thoughts

An individual's mental health is a combination of overall well-being, including physical, mental, and social well-being and exposure to a variety of risk factors such as violence, economic pressure, and stress can have a detrimental effect on mental health. Research shows that more than 50% of individuals will be diagnosed with a mental illness or disorder, approximately 44 million adults experience a mental illness in any one year, and approximately 9.8 million adults live with a serious mental illness.

Unfortunately, poor mental health not only affects adults, but also youth. Out of the 50 million plus public school students in the United States, approximately 21.4% of 13-18-year-old teens and 13% of 8-15-year-old children experience a severe mental health disorder, potentially depriving them of the opportunity to learn and build the necessary relationships for their social well-being. It is staggering to realize that 80% of the students that are affected by mental health problems will not receive counseling, therapy, medication, or any treatment at all. Research has also shown that there is a rise in mental health among college-aged students due, in part, to the greater levels of stress they are under.

Although research shows that correlation and causality are complicated, there is an association among individuals within the adult prison system and youth in the juvenile justice system with mental illness. Individuals committed to the United States prison system with mental illness have significantly increased with up to 24% of prisoners having a mental health condition. Of the two million youth in the juvenile system, 70% have at least one mental health condition and at least 20% have a serious mental illness, a rate three times higher than the general youth population.

For individuals that seek and are able to receive treatment, the number of psychiatric drug prescriptions are surging across the globe, potentially contributing to the rise in mental health issues as many of the drugs (along with recreational drugs) worsen, bring about symptoms of mental illness, and/or cause addiction, a mental health disease in and of itself.

**Points to Remember**

- *Mental illness is different from an individual's well-being and mental health in that mental illness is comprised of a variety of acute or chronic conditions that affect a person's thinking, feeling, mood and/or behavior.*
- *In the United States, Massachusetts, Vermont, Maine, Minnesota, North Dakota, and Delaware have the lowest incidences of mental illness in the country as they have the best access to insurance and responsive mental health treatment programs.*
- *Factors that can influence an individual's risk for mental illness include early adverse life experiences, such as trauma and abuse, biological factors, such as genes or chemical imbalances in the brain, the use of alcohol or recreational drugs.*
- *Mental disorders affect an estimated 300 million individuals worldwide with an estimated 60 million individuals diagnosed with bipolar, 23 million with schizophrenia, and 50 million with dementia. Mood disorders, such as major depression, are the third most common cause of hospitalization in the United States for both youth and adults; it is anticipated that by 2030, depression will be the number one cause of disease burden across the world.*
- *Adults living with mental health issues who do not seek or receive treatment consume approximately 38% of all alcohol, 44% of all cocaine, and 40% of all cigarettes as a form of self-medication.*

# Chapter Two

# In Pursuit of Improved Therapeutic Outcomes: Understanding the Potency of Evidence-Based Practices

The interest in evidence-based practices (EBPs) in psychotherapy has exploded in recent times. For patients with specific profiles, EBPs have shown promise to deliver better and faster results than standard treatment options (i.e., talk therapy, medication, etc.). EBPs have shown both strengths and challenges in practice and are also fraught with misconceptions about their use and the types of patients for whom they show the most success. As a treatment option for certain psychological disorders, EBPs may be beneficial for patients who prefer psychotherapy to traditional pharmacological treatment options (McHugh, Whitton, Peckham, Welge, & Otto, 2013). Despite the overall acceptance of EBPs in the psychological community, there is a lack of widespread use among practicing therapists. Examining EBPs holistically may provide the answer as to how to use them with more fidelity, as well as to ensure they are tailored to meet the needs of patients both pre- and post-treatment (Cooks, Schwartz, & Kaslow, 2017).

## Defining Evidence-Based Practices (EBPs)

As evidence-based treatment in medicine moved to the forefront of research in the 1990s, so too did the idea of evidence-based psychotherapy practices (Cook et al., 2017). In 2005, the American Psychiatric Association (APA) developed guidelines around EBPs in psychotherapy after they adapted the following definition of EBPs from Sackett, Straus, Richardson, Rosenberg and Haynes (2000): "the integration of best research evidence with clinical expertise and patient values" (p. 147).

It was upon this definition that the guidelines were and still are based today. The evidence upon which these practices are based comes from research, including analyses of studies, randomized controlled trials, and case studies. From this evidence, practitioners are tasked with considering patient profiles, along with developing effective treatment plans in line with practice guidelines (Cook et al., 2017). Clinicians must choose the EBP that they think will be most effective for their client based on a variety of factors, and much of the evidence suggests that EBPs are more effective than treatment-as-usual for the majority of patients in psychotherapy (Weisz, Ugueto, Cheron, & Herren, 2013).

The goals of EBPs are twofold. First, EBPs purport to increase the quality of care for patients, as well as increasing accountability so that patients are only subjected to treatments that have been proven successful over numerous replicated studies (Selva, 2018). Second, EPBs are professed to be a more cost-effective treatment for patients, based on the claim that clients will spend less time in treatment than patients undergoing treatment-as-usual (Selva, 2018). There are numerous EBPs in the psychotherapy world, some with better outcomes for specific types of patients. There is evidence, for example, that the use of EBPs for youths with mild to moderate conditions has a more positive effect on treatment outcomes than treatment-as-usual (Weisz et al., 2013).

Equally as important, some EBPs work best for specific modalities of treatment. EBPs that target such conditions as eating disorders and substance abuse disorders work best in a group therapy model, whereas patients suffering from depression have a likely higher rate of success when treated with EBPs in individual counseling sessions.

**Strengths and Challenges of EBPs in Practice**

When looking into treatment options for patients, therapists often look at whether or not a practice has significant evidence backing up its validity and effectiveness. Relying on practices that have a strong evidence-based backing makes sense for therapists, as opposed to using standard practices that cannot be supported with the same degree of certainty. Talk therapy, for example, while important in treating many patients, cannot be replicated with the same degree of fidelity in all patients. EBPs, on the other hand, generally have more robust guidelines and tools that can be applied to a multitude of patients with the same type of consistency (Cook et al., 2017). And while fidelity to treatment method is key in the success of the EBP, these practices have the flexibility to be adapted in order to individualize patient treatment. Therapists have the ability to determine the most appropriate way in which to incorporate an EBP into practice based on the patient's unique profile (Barends & Briner, 2014).

Another benefit of utilizing EBPs in practice is that they are cost-effective and save time in treatment. Using treatment-as-usual methods, such as a combination of talk therapy and medication, can often take years for patients to show substantial improvement. Not only does this cost the patient and therapist valuable time, but it also takes a toll on the patient's wallet. In cases where the patient cannot afford treatment or has a lapse in insurance, the effects can be detrimental to progress. Yet in the case of EBPs, patients often learn skills that can carry over into everyday life and be used consistently even in the absence of direct treatment (Patitz, Anderson, & Navajits, 2015).

While it appears that there is a promise of greater effectiveness for EBPs, it is necessary to consider the challenges associated with their use. One such challenge is the question of whether or not EBPs can be generalized considering that much of the evidence upon which these practices are based was obtained through randomized control studies, which differ dramatically from real-world patient scenarios (Cook et al., 2017; Kazdin, 2008). Treatment outcomes for patients who have a variety of external influences impacting their conditions, or who have comorbid conditions are not likely to be known through the existing research on EBPs. Patients with complex treatment needs are also at a disadvantage in benefitting from EBP treatment simply due to the fact that the success of such treatment on this population is not well-known (Kazdin, 2008).

A majority of patients who seek out psychotherapy do so in order to help them cope with the daily stressors of life (Cook et al., 2017). Treatment-as-usual can help patients to improve their condition with less focus on the rigid adherence to a treatment plan and more focus on self-improvement over time. This leads to another challenge as the wide range of patients who seek psychotherapy for conditions that haven't risen to the clinical level do not benefit from EBPs. Most EBPs focus on very targeted methods of treating the symptoms of specific disorders, are based on cognitive-behavioral models, and do not incorporate other modalities of therapy, such as systemic, integrative, or humanistic (Emmelkamp et al., 2014).

A final challenge with EBPs is that they are often overused. Therapists who rely on the strictness of any manualized program risk ignoring their own professional judgment. In some patients, the human-centered method of treating the condition far outweighs the reliance on a programmatic treatment; therefore, for therapists who may tend to rely heavily on the rules of an EBP may be better off sticking with treatment-as-usual options. Over-reliance on EBPs rules can ultimately result in the questionable effectiveness of the program. In some patients, a more flexible approach is needed to help promote treatment progress. For patients whose therapists strictly follow the EBP plan, they may experience success in one facet of their treatment, but overall may not reach desired outcomes (Cook et al., 2017; Greenhalgh, Howick, & Maskrey, 2014).

**Misconceptions of EBPs and their Effectiveness**

As wide-spread as EBPs seem to be, many therapists are reluctant to use them as a primary means of treatment for their patients. This is perhaps due to the many misconceptions of EBP use and outcomes. One of the main misconceptions of EBPs is that they are merely manualized programs that do not allow for individual therapist judgment (Cook et al., 2017). Many therapists fear that a reliance on oversimplified treatments will lead to ineffective outcomes for their clients; however, the American Psychological Association (2005) suggested that therapists who use EBPs should incorporate their own clinical expertise into practice. As the response to EBPs varies depending upon the patient's individual profile, so too should the therapists' approach to applying the techniques provided in the selected EBP.

It is more appropriate to consider EBPs as a guideline for therapists rather than a set-in-stone roadmap of how to treat a client. Flexibility is key in providing treatment that is both individualized for the patient and adherent to the goals of the EBP. Remaining faithful to the guidelines of the EBP is critical in providing treatment that can be replicated with similar levels of effectiveness, yet enough flexibility must be incorporated into treatment to account for patients' unique needs and circumstances. Therapists should choose an EBP that is appropriate for the patient/modality and strive to retain the core components of the EBP in practice (Cook et al., 2017).

Another misconception about EBPs is that they ignore patients' actual needs in favor of strict, cost-cutting measures. In theory, EBPs can provide a more cost-effective means of treatment by reducing the number of treatment sessions for clients, and there has been evidence suggesting this is true for certain patients; however, therapists cannot ignore the humanistic approach to providing counseling to clients, and must always consider the client's values, preferences, and circumstances (Patitz et al., 2015). Cook et al. (2017) suggested that incorporating EBPs and the therapist's own clinical expertise often creates the most effective means of treatment for clients, which also results in the greatest cost-effective measures.

Many therapists feel as though traditional therapy methods cannot compete with EBPs. Traditional methods, such as talk therapy, often lack the evidence base of EBPs. As previously stated, talk therapy has its benefits but is often a slower method of treatment than most EBPs and can have inconsistent results for patients; however, studies have shown mixed results with regard to the effectiveness of treatment-as-usual versus traditional therapy (Weisz et al., 2013). There doesn't appear to be sufficient evidence to firmly theorize that EBPs have a greater impact on treatment outcomes than traditional therapy over time.

Another aspect of traditional therapy that should be considered is that EBPs have not been adequately studied in all subgroups of patients; for instance, little is known about the effectiveness of EBPs for use by school psychologists (Zaboski, Schrack, Joyce-Beaulieu, & MacIness, 2017). For this particular subgroup of clients, treatment options should vary between traditional methods and specifically chosen aspects of EBPs. A holistic approach to treatment, for example, takes into consideration the influence of community, family, school, personality, and the individual's development should be contemplated (Nissen, 2011).

## Applying EBPs: Considerations for Treatment

It is clear that there are many factors to consider when determining the likely effectiveness of incorporating an EBP into treatment; however, aside from the specific characteristics of EBPs that may or may not make them effective, further research suggests that there are additional factors impacting the success or failure of EBPs for increased treatment outcomes. Outside of the evidence upon which the practice is based, the patient's relationship with the provider, the flexibility in treatment planning, the fidelity to the core components of the EBP, the context of the treatment, and even the profile of the provider can have important impacts upon the effectiveness of the EBP (Cook et al., 2017).

## The Relationship Between Patient and Therapist

The relationship between a patient and therapist is critical for developing a successful treatment plan. The more compatible the patient and provider are with each other, the more likely treatment outcomes will be positive (Norcross & Wampold, 2011). Together with treatment methods and the patient's individual profile, the relationship can often influence patients to stick with treatment or to follow through with using learned strategies in real-world situations outside of therapy. As the therapist looks for the most appropriate EBP, consideration must be given to how solid the relationship is between the therapist and the client. The therapist must be able to adapt the relationship to the client's needs, which can further improve treatment outcomes (Norcross & Wampold, 2011).

In addition to the therapist's relationship with the patient, the patient must also have a positive relationship with other patients (in the case of group therapy), family members, and/or peers (Cook et al., 2017). These influences can make or break a patient's treatment success; for instance, patients who have a solid support system (both in and outside of therapy), concrete goals, as well as ways to collaborate with others on those goals, generally show more success in treatment outcomes (Norcross & Wampold, 2011).

In order to ensure an effective working relationship with patients, therapists must examine the EBP treatment guidelines and determine how they best fit with the desired outcome of treatment given the patient/therapist relationship. As previously stated, therapists must prioritize the patient's individual needs over the manualized guidelines of any EBP. That being said, therapists must demonstrate that they have their client's best interests in mind when choosing a therapeutic intervention, and truly base their choice on the individual facets of the patient's profile. In doing so, therapists must be willing to collaborate with patients, creating a two-way street for treatment and recovery (Levitt, Pomerville, & Surface, 2016).

**Fidelity of Implementation**

As mentioned earlier, therapists who remain faithful to EBP core components generally have patients who experience more positive treatment outcomes. In EBPs, core components are the basic structural elements of the program and are required in order to maintain the validity of the practice. Utilizing the core components as guidelines by which treatment is offered can be much more effective than insisting that patients fit into the rules of standardized practice (Cook et al., 2017). The point is for the therapist to implement the EBP to closely resemble its original intent, while maintaining the flexibility to change the treatment as necessary to fit the patient's need. When an EBP no longer maintains most of the components upon which the research is based, it then fails to be an EBP (Cook et al., 2017).

**Flexibility in Practice**

Any successful therapist can concur that flexibility in practice is key in providing appropriate care for patients; however, flexibility in EBP use may not only refer to reducing the number of prescribed sessions, or changes in individual applications of treatment. Flexibility also refers to altering the timeframe over which treatment is scheduled to be provided (Chung, 2014). An EBP that is scheduled to take 10 sessions of treatment may actually take 20 sessions if the therapist feels that a mix of traditional therapy and EBPs are needed to adequately meet the patient's needs (Swales, 2009). A change in the therapy modality may also be needed. Many EBPs have shown success in specific modalities. Mindfulness-Based Cognitive Therapy (MBCT) has been shown most successful in group therapy, while Dialectical Behavior Therapy (DBT) has demonstrated greater success rates in individual sessions (Swales, 2009; Witkiewitz & Bowen, 2010). For patients who have difficulty making it to a therapy session, options such as e-therapy or telephone sessions may be needed.

Therapists should be flexible enough to recognize which modality may be best for a specific patient; yet, they must also be mindful of fidelity with the EBP. A delicate balance of flexibility and fidelity is needed to ensure that the therapist is maintaining the key components of the EBP, while providing enough flexibility to meet the patients where they are. This is why it is necessary for therapists using EBPs to be able to teach transferable skills to patients who may need unique accommodations. Patients who can only inconsistently attend therapy sessions, for example, may not benefit from treatment unless the EBP provides the therapist ways in which to teach coping strategies in a short amount of time that can be generalized into the patient's life outside of therapy (Swales, 2009; Witkiewitz & Bowen, 2010).

## Context

The context in which therapy is provided has an impact upon its effectiveness. One particularly challenging area for the provision of therapy (traditional and EBPs) is the school setting. While there are numerous EBPs in practice for students with a variety of needs, such as suicidal ideation, autism spectrum disorder, and anxiety, there are challenges with providing continued and effective treatment (Commonwealth of Virginia: Commission on Youth, 2017). EBPs can be costly at the start, both for the program materials and for training of staff. This is often a major barrier for schools that wish to broaden their treatment options (Cook et al., 2017). There may also be challenges surrounding when treatment is provided during the school day and how often treatment is provided, as well as student attendance rates that will impact efficacy. These are all factors to consider when contemplating EBP use in this particular context (Schaeffer et al., 2005; Zaboski et al., 2017).

Another important aspect to consider about context is that many EBPs are designed to treat one specific condition; however, the reality is that many patients suffer from co-morbid conditions that require a multitude of treatments (Cook et al., 2017). There are some EBPs that do address co-occurring conditions, such as the Seeking Safety program (Treatment Innovations, 2016), which treats co-morbid trauma and substance abuse disorder. Functional family therapy (FFT) can be adapted to treat substance abuse and conduct disorder, while working to restore family relationships (Chung et al., 2014; Datchi & Sexton, 2013). It is necessary for therapists to critically examine which EBP has the likely ability to be effective for patients who suffer from multiple conditions. Therapists should also not be afraid to choose traditional therapy options over EBPs if they feel as though the EBP will not be effective.

**Provider Profile**

In reality, there are many types of providers who practice EBPs. Just as there are many modalities and contexts within which EBPs are used, there are as many different providers who utilize EBPs. Psychotherapists are a small portion of professionals who use these practices; physicians, nurses, social workers, school counselors, and graduate students can all be providers of EBPs (Cook et al., 2017).

Patients who are seeking a professional who practices EBPs should consider the therapist's training, clinical experience, and attitude toward EBPs. A factor in EBP effectiveness is the provider's experience in using the practice. For therapists who have had direct training in an EBP, it is likely that their patients will have better outcomes than those of providers who have not had such training.

## Final Thoughts

In order for EBPs to become more widely used by therapists, the knowledge base of their implementation must be increased across the field. Training for providers, along with more research on EBP effectiveness may help increase EBP acceptance and use for a variety of disorders; however, as more research results become available, it is likely that EBPs will become the standard of treatment for therapists looking to increase patient outcomes, as well as save patients money and time (Cook et al., 2017).

The future research on EBPs must focus on external influences such as socio-demographics, interpersonal relationships with families and peers, and patient self-concept (Hunnicutt Hollenbaugh, 2011). These, among other factors, play a critical role in the effectiveness of any therapeutic intervention. Researchers may consider examining the effectiveness of EBPs in conjunction with pharmacological interventions for patients who require both forms of treatment in order to experience success (McHugh et al., 2013). Continued collaboration from researchers and practicing therapists will likely yield the most positive outcomes in the development of future EBPs.

## Points to Remember

- *As a treatment option for certain psychological disorders, EBPs may be beneficial for patients who prefer psychotherapy to traditional pharmacological treatment options.*
- *EBPs integrate current research with clinical expertise as it relates to the culture and characteristics of the patient.*
- *There are many strengths and challenges to EBP use, and therapists must overcome the misconceptions of the effectiveness of EBPs in order to begin to use them with fidelity.*
- *Outside of the evidence upon which EBPs are based, the patient's relationship with their provider, the therapist's flexibility in treatment planning, the therapist's fidelity to the core components of the EBP, the context of the treatment, and even the profile of the provider can have important impacts upon the effectiveness of the EBP.*
- *More research is needed on EBP effectiveness, specifically with regard to their use in conjunction with pharmacological interventions.*

# Chapter Three
# Promoting Positive Change One Client at a Time: Evidenced-Based Individual Therapy Practices

As treatment modalities go, individual therapy is the most widely practiced form of psychotherapy in existence. This is likely due to the personalized nature of the treatment, as well as the ability for therapists to help with a plethora of mental health conditions such as anxiety, depression, substance abuse, school difficulties, marital problems, and life transitions (California State University Channel Islands [CSUCI], 2019).

Individual counseling is perhaps best known for its reliance on talk therapy as a means of treatment, in which patients are able to work with the therapist one-on-one to process through issues that impact their thoughts, behaviors, and feelings (CSUCI, 2019). Therapists generally work with patients to develop treatment goals, and many client concerns can be addressed with short-term therapy. Not everyone who seeks counseling suffers from mental illness. There are many individuals who pursue counseling services to help them to cope with life transitions, negative thought patterns, and even insomnia (Mayo Clinic, 2019).

Research has indicated that psychotherapy is most effective for conditions such as depression and anxiety, resulting in fewer relapses into more serious forms of these disorders. As a matter of fact, it has been reported that psychotherapy has a greater impact on reducing client relapse than pharmacological interventions on their own (CSUCI, 2019). With so many evidence-based therapies available for clinicians to implement, more and more therapists who treat individual patients are relying on these treatment methods to increase their client outcomes.

For patients who suffer from more difficult to treat conditions with a high likelihood of relapse, such as borderline personality disorder, EBPs have shown the greatest impact on treatment outcomes (MacPherson, Cheavens, & Fristad, 2013; Masino Drass, 2015; Neacsiu, Ward-Ciesielski, & Linehan, 2012; Swales, 2009). Patients who suffer from depression, suicidal ideation and non-suicidal self-injurious behavior are more often helped over the long term by EBPs in individual therapy practice (Pistorello, Fruzzetti, MacLane, Gallop, & Iverson, 2012).

Individual therapy also boasts some of the best-known EBPs in practice. Four of the most commonly-used EBPs in individual therapy – cognitive behavior therapy, dialectical behavior therapy, exposure therapy, and mindfulness-based cognitive therapy – are also the most well-studied (MacPherson et al., 2013; Pistorello et al., 2012). These EBPs can be used for a wide variety of mental health challenges; however, like all other EBPs, there are specific conditions for which they were designed and with which they show the most success. As with all EBPs, it is necessary for the therapist to consider which client profiles are likely to see the most success when choosing an appropriate EBP.

## Client and Therapist Characteristics to Consider

As with any form of therapy, client and therapist characteristics can impact the success of treatment. It would seem as though individuals who actively seek out treatment would be driven to work toward alleviating the symptoms of their respective condition; however, the client's individual characteristics can influence treatment outcomes just as much as the treatment method. Patients who are engaged and willing to participate in treatment may not always fare better with intervention than those who are reluctant to attend sessions (Groth-Marnet, Roberts, & Beutler, 2001). Several client and therapist characteristics to consider include the client's expectation of treatment, therapist's personality, client's motivation, and ability for the client and therapist to form a positive therapeutic alliance.

### Expectation of Treatment

Client expectations are key to the success of psychotherapy. These expectations can influence the client's decision to enter into therapy, remain there, and work to complete the intervention. Clients must also have the belief that they can be successful, and that the therapist truly cares about their outcomes (Patterson, Uhlin, & Anderson, 2008). Although the research on client expectations in therapy outcomes is limited, there is research that suggests that patients who expect to have positive outcomes often do, while patients who expect to have negative outcomes are likely to drop out of treatment (Patterson et al., 2008).

Patients who expect to form a strong working relationship with their therapist are more likely to put forth the effort needed to follow through with treatment.

## Therapist Personality

For patients who observe therapists be honest, trustworthy, caring, open, and warm, there is likely to be a better working relationship than for patients who view their therapist with cynicism (Chapman, Talbot, Tatman, & Brition 2009). Therapists must maintain a balancing act between being approachable, yet firm when it comes to helping clients progress through treatment. A therapist who is too lax will likely end up with patients who fail to follow through with treatment work, miss sessions, and show little improvement overall. Conversely, a therapist who is too strict may end up with the same type of patient as the lax therapist, but due to the patient's discomfort with the therapist's rigidity, or fear of judgment for not making greater strides in treatment.

## Client Motivation

In order for any type of therapy to be successful, clients must be motivated to change. The more a client is motivated through a personal agency, the more effective treatment will be (Chen-Lin & Yun, 2016). Client motivation enhances the outcome of EBPs because clients who are motivated are more likely to consistently attend treatment sessions in sequence. Clients who demonstrate the most motivation are usually those who report noticing that treatment is effective long before the intervention actually ends.

## Therapist/Client Alliances

Evidence suggests that clients who fail to form strong alliances with their therapists are more likely to experience higher dropout rates from treatment (Cox, 2017; Patterson et al., 2008). The therapeutic alliance refers to the relationship that is developed over time between the patient and therapist. A study by Horvath, Del Re, Fluckiger, & Symonds (2011) indicated that after examining over 4,000 cases, the alliance between patient and therapist was the single most important factor influencing treatment outcomes across all modalities. The alliance can be boiled down to three components (1) agreement on therapy goals, (2) agreement on tasks of therapy, and (3) the emotional connection between the therapist and the client (Cox, 2017). If there is a rift between the client and therapist over any of these components, treatment outcomes can suffer.

## Evidence-Based Approaches for Individual Therapy

Individual therapy is perhaps the most practiced modality among psychotherapists; therefore, there has been significant research on EBPs in this area. Much of the recent research in the area of individual therapy has been in the areas of dialectical behavior therapy (DBT), cognitive behavior therapy (CBT), exposure therapy, and mindfulness-based cognitive therapy (MBCT) (Benjamin et al., 2011). These therapies often combine cognitive, behavioral, developmental, and social theories of human behavior into an integrated model of treatment (Benjamin et al., 2011).

Research on the outcomes of these EBPs generally show positive results, yet like other forms of therapy, certain therapies work best with specific client profiles and disorders (Rizvi, 2011). Regardless of the EBP, the goal of these treatments is to change client behavior through developing more positive replacement behaviors, which will ultimately result in a reduction in maladaptive and problematic behavior.

### Cognitive Behavior Therapy (CBT)

CBT is a form of therapy that aims to reframe negative thought patterns and subsequent behaviors. CBT is often the first-line treatment for post-traumatic stress disorder, and it usually consists of imagined scenarios as well as real-life exposure to traumatic memories so that cognitive restructuring around these experiences can take place (Felmingham & Bryant, 2012).

CBT is based on the cognitive model of emotional response, suggesting that patients can change the way they act based on more positive thinking (National Association of Cognitive-Behavioral Therapists, n.d.). CBT itself is not a distinct therapeutic model; there are several therapies that use CBT as a base, including dialectical behavior therapy. That being said, CBT and its similar therapies share many of the same characteristics to include

- CBT is designed to be brief and time-limited: CBT is considered one of the most rapid forms of treatment, with the average number of sessions being approximately 16. CBT is highly instructive, and it provides clients with homework assignments that they are required to do on their own to enhance treatment outcomes. The decision to discontinue treatment is a mutual decision by both patient and therapist.
- A strong therapeutic alliance, while helpful, is not the focus of treatment: Therapists believe that clients get better over time not because of the relationship between client and therapist;

rather, it occurs when clients have learned to change their ways of thinking.
- CBT is collaborative: The therapist and client work together to achieve the client's goals. The role of the therapist is to listen, guide, and teach; yet, the majority of the work falls on the client to implement what has been learned.
- CBT does not tell clients how to feel: While most clients seeking therapy are looking to change some negative emotions and/or behavior, CBT emphasizes calmness in the face of undesirable situations. It also emphasizes accepting a problem and making a knowledgeable decision about how to solve it without an overreliance on emotions.
- CBT encourages clients to use self-questioning: Therapists ask clients about how they are feeling and why they may be feeling that way. They also encourage clients to use self-questioning to work through their feelings, as well as to develop alternative perspectives on a problematic situation.
- CBT is structured and directed: In a CBT session, therapists do not tell their clients what their goals should be, nor how they should feel. Instead, therapists teach clients how they should behave in order to achieve a specific goal.
- CBT is based on an educational model: CBT is based on the assumption that emotions and behaviors are learned and can, therefore, be unlearned. The goal of CBT is to help the client unlearn negative reactions, while relearning more productive ways of dealing with a problem (National Association of Cognitive-Behavioral Therapists, n.d.).

**Program structure.** Since the goal of CBT is to build a skill set that helps the patient become aware of their thoughts and emotions, while changing ways of thinking that continue to exacerbate a pattern of negative or unwanted behaviors and emotions, therapists combine in-person therapy sessions with homework assignments that are completed by the patient (National Association of Cognitive-Behavioral Therapists, n.d.). CBT is designed to be provided over a shorter period of time than other therapies, typically between 12 and 20 sessions depending on the client's condition and the treatment needed.

Cully & Teten (2008), suggested one type of structure for the program. The first session should be dedicated to orienting the patient to CBT, assessing the patient's concerns, and setting initial treatment goals. The following sessions should focus on beginning and providing intervention techniques until the final sessions, where the therapist helps the patient prepare for sustaining changes outside of therapy (Cully & Teten, 2008).

CBT is suitable for many conditions; however, the intensity of treatment may vary. Phobias, chronic PTSD, and alcohol dependence would not be successfully treated with a brief set of sessions. For conditions such as those, a longer, more intensive treatment model of CBT would likely be helpful (Cully & Teten, 2008). When choosing the model of CBT, therapists should consider the likelihood of a strong working relationship that could be forged quickly, the probability that the patient will follow through with homework assignments, and the severity of the patient's condition.

**Treatment outcomes.** CBT has been widely studied and supported as an effective treatment method for a variety of conditions in a multitude of settings. Recent studies indicate promising results for groups that have not been previously studied extensively with the use of CBT (Vandervord Nixon, Sterk, & Pearce, 2012; Wong et al., 2018). A study on the effectiveness of CBT with adolescents suffering from anxiety problems in Hong Kong had encouraging initial results; however, there was no noted difference between experimental and control groups with regard to positive changes in cognition – both groups demonstrated positive growth (Wong et al., 2018). That is not to say that CBT was not effective for the group in this study; rather, other factors may have influenced control group improvements (Wong et al., 2018).

A study on the effect of CBT on the effect of childhood PTSD resulted in 91% of participants who completed treatment as no longer suffering from PTSD-related symptoms (Vandervord Nixon et al., 2012). They cited similar studies that supported their findings in which 92% of children lose the diagnosis of PTSD altogether by posttreatment. In a study on adults with PTSD, Felmingham & Bryant (2012) discovered that CBT is effective for both men and women; yet, has a more substantial effect on men over the long-term with PTSD reduction. Although these studies are small in scope, they add to the existing body of literature supporting CBT effectiveness on various conditions and with a multitude of patient profiles.

**Dialectical Behavior Therapy (DBT)**

DBT combines classical and operant conditioning through the analysis of client behavior. Therapists examine the ways in which the clients have been conditioned by their environment, peers, etc., to engage in target behaviors, and they seek to understand how the problematic behavior works to serve a purpose for the client (Swales, 2009). The goal of DBT is to decrease problematic behaviors while increasing the acquisition and generalization of healthy behaviors.

DBT was designed as a treatment for patients suffering from borderline personality disorder (BPD). These patients exhibited chronic suicidal ideations and were often much more difficult to treat due to either the rate at which they followed through with suicide or the amount of time they were hospitalized for psychiatric complaints such as depression and anxiety (Rizvi, 2011). Patients with BPD often have high therapy dropout rates, which is a contributing factor to treatment difficulty.

As success was seen with patients suffering from borderline personality disorder, DBT grew to treat a variety of other mental health conditions, including adolescents and elderly patients who present with suicidal ideation, adults with eating disorders, oppositional children, victims of domestic abuse, and difficult-to-treat correctional patients (Neacsiu et al., 2012). Research has continued to support DBT's effectiveness across populations and with various client profiles (MacPherson et al., 2013; Neacsiu et al., 2012; Pistorello et al., 2012).

**Program structure.** DBT is a comprehensive program that can be used across several modalities, including individual, group, and the therapist consultation model. The treatment is based on a dialectical worldview that consists of three overarching principles: 1) No event in the universe can be understood outside of its context and as part of the whole; 2) each patient's interpretation of reality has a polar opposite interpretation; and 3) continuous movement is necessary in treatment (Neacsiu et al. 2012). DBT recognizes the need to consider the patient and personal circumstances holistically as influencing the condition. Chapman (2006) provided an overview of the five functions of treatment when using DBT.

1. The first function is to enhance the patient's skills in basic life skills. For instance, patients in DBT may have trouble regulating emotions, so helping these patients to develop these skills is useful in helping to lessen negative behaviors that stem from emotional dysregulation.
2. The first function segues into the second of DBT, generalizing capabilities, which allows the patient to successfully transfer the skills built in therapy into the real world. Patients are provided with homework which directs them to practice skills in a variety of situations. Therapists provide support in between sessions, especially when the patient is faced with an increasingly difficult situation in which professional guidance may be required.

3. The third function of treatment – improving motivation and reducing dysfunctional behaviors – involves improving client motivation to make positive changes while at the same time reducing behaviors that negatively impact the client's goals. In between therapy sessions, clients are instructed to track dysfunctional behavior by time and occurrence. Therapists prioritize these behaviors, focusing on self-harming behaviors first. The practitioner then helps the client to discover the reasoning behind the negative behavior, as well as the consequences that are potentially reinforcing the behavior.
4. Therapists must structure the environment of their treatment to be sure it reinforces or promotes positive progress, making this the fourth function of DBT. This method can help patients also learn ways to modify their own environments; for instance, moving away from people or places that trigger negative behavior.
5. Therapists accomplish the previous four functions through the last function of DBT, which is enhancing their own capabilities and motivation. Treating patients with such complex conditions can be challenging; therefore, it is necessary for therapists to participate in continued training while obtaining the support of therapists treating similarly.

**Treatment outcomes.** DBT is used in a variety of modalities and with a multitude of conditions; therefore, treatment outcomes vary. Generally, studies have indicated positive outcomes with DBT in comparison to other forms of therapy; for example, Pistorello et al. (2012) conducted a randomized clinical trial of 63 college students seeking assistance at a college counseling center. This research suggested that DBT has the ability to be adapted to treat college students with various complex conditions, including those who presented with suicidal ideation (Pistorello et al., 2012). Students who participated in DBT showed improvements in depression baseline scores and showed no worsening in suicidality as opposed to students receiving treatment as usual. Although the study was small in scope, it suggested that DBT is effective and safe for treating clients with complex and severe conditions within a college counseling model (Pistorello et al., 2012).

In a review of studies on the use of DBT with adolescents, MacPherson et al. (2013) discovered that in adolescents with oppositional defiance disorder (ODD), behavior disorder (BD), eating disorders, and trichotillomania (hair pulling), promising results from treatment occurred. Although the studies examined differed in treatment length and setting, most patients reported reduced symptoms over a period of time (MacPherson et al., 2013). Significant improvements have been noted in patients' ability to function outside of treatment, as well as their ability to generalize treatment into novel situations.

Rizvi (2011) suggested that while the majority of evidence on DBT is positive, not all patients experience success with this method of treatment. Rizvi (2011) suggests that when one facet of the treatment link breaks, treatment failure is likely. DBT success is impacted by factors such as the severity of the client's disorder, the severity of symptoms, and the likelihood that they will follow through with treatment. Positive treatment outcomes are often low as BPD is notoriously difficult to treat.

When measuring treatment success or failure within the DBT model, the treatment itself states that it is impossible for the client to fail. It is both the therapist's and treatment's responsibility to promote positive outcomes for the client; therefore, it is likely easier to measure the number of patients who successfully complete treatment as opposed to those who treatment has failed.

For patients with BPD, it may be necessary to examine other forms of treatment that utilize a DBT framework; for example, in a few limited studies, art therapy has shown promise for patients with BPD (Masino Drass, 2015). While not explicitly DBT, art therapy uses aspects of DBT to promote coping skills in order to help patients establish safety, identify emotions, and commit to strategies that will ultimately help reduce maladaptive behaviors.

**Mindfulness-Based Cognitive Therapy (MBCT)**

MCBT is a form of therapy that incorporates elements of CBT with mindfulness-based stress reduction. The program was initially designed to help patients prevent relapse with recurrent forms of depression but has more recently been utilized to treat various other psychiatric conditions (Sipe & Eisendrath, 2012). The focus of MBCT is to encourage patients to develop new and healthy ways of relating to their thoughts and feelings instead of forcing change in cognitive patterns.

MBCT is primarily a clinical intervention that uses the principles of mindfulness to support clients in developing different thought patterns (USCD Center for Mindfulness, 2019b). Mindfulness refers to the process that promotes nonjudgmental awareness in the present state (Hoffman, Sawyer, Witt, & Oh, 2010; Kabat-Zinn, 2005). Characteristics of mindfulness include noticing physical sensations, thoughts, bodily awareness, and the environment.

There are two states of mindfulness that patients can practice. The first encourages patients to self-regulate their attention through the focus on one outside stimulus, such as breathing or a mantra; while the second is characterized by focusing on the present moment with curiosity, openness, and acceptance (Hoffman et al., 2010). The basic premise of mindfulness practice is that when a client experiences the present moment, just as it is, they can learn to counter internal stressors that lead to irrational and negative behavior (Green & Bieling, 2012).

**Program structure.** Generally speaking, MBCT is provided over a brief period of time, usually 8 weekly sessions in which participants are taught the techniques of mindfulness that helps them to become aware of how changes happen in their minds and bodies when they feel a certain emotion or think a specific thought. In addition to mindfulness training, MBCT includes aspects of CBT to help patients learn ways in which to rewire their thought processes that cause them to react negatively to emotions and thoughts (Institute for Mindfulness-Based Approaches, 2019).

Much like CBT, each MBCT session is designed to address the goal of becoming independent of treatment, with the ability to practice mindfulness techniques on one's own. Patients are also provided with homework in MBCT, which helps them to continue practicing the tenets of the program to reinforce what is learned in session.

**Treatment outcomes.** Because MBCT is an increasingly popular form of therapy for such conditions as anxiety and depression, its effects have been widely studied. Most studies indicate that MBCT is an effective treatment option for these conditions. In a study on treatment-resistant depression, Eisendrath, Chartier, & McLane (2011) discovered that MBCT had positive effects on reducing the recurrence of depression symptoms that had not responded to pharmacological treatment.

Once patients were able to master mindfulness techniques, they were more likely to notice the positive effects of treatment. As a side effect, increased focus and concentration in everyday life has also been suggested. The study did note that one potential roadblock to success is session attendance and willingness to follow through with homework; however, in patients motivated to change, the reduction in depression relapse is likely (USCD Center for Mindfulness, 2019a).

Other similar studies reported successful outcomes for MBCT. Huijbers, Spinhoven, van Schaik, Nolen, & Speckens (2016) reported that patients who relied on medication therapy for depression performed equally well in MBCT when examining the reduction and recurrence of symptoms. Similarly, Green & Bieling (2012) noted that patients who participated in eight-week MCBT sessions demonstrated a decrease in mood symptoms, total number of perceived life stressors, and perceived severity of those stressors.

In a meta-analysis of studies on mindfulness-based therapies (including MBCT and mindfulness-based stress reduction), Hoffman et al. (2010) discovered that findings indicate success among populations that utilize these therapies to treat anxiety and depression. MCBT has also shown promise in treating certain types of phobias. In a study on social anxiety disorder among college students, Brady & Whitman (2011), discovered that symptoms of this disorder may improve in as little as four sessions of MBCT.

**Exposure Therapy**

Exposure therapy is a treatment developed to help people confront their fears by slowly incorporating exposure to the fearful object, situation, or activity (American Psychiatric Association, n.d.). Typically, when people fear something or someone, they avoid interaction at all costs. Even though this avoidance can help over the short-term, it rarely produces long-term results insofar as helping the person become immune to the fear caused. In fact, avoidance can exacerbate fear as the mind generates unsavory scenarios involving the fear that are often worse than simply confronting the fear (American Psychiatric Association, n.d.)

Exposing clients to objects and situations they would normally choose to avoid can provide several benefits. Exposure therapy can reduce client sensitivities to stressors that can be perceived as threatening. It can help to weaken the connection between stimuli and negative outcomes; for example, associating a creaking floor with someone intending to do harm may not always be a rational thought (Lustbader, 2019).

Exposure therapy can provide the client with alternative ways of thinking about the creaking floor, such as 'the building is settling' or 'the house is old.' This helps the client to recognize other perspectives that can rationalize away fear. Clients can also learn to co-exist with fear as a natural response to certain environmental changes. This is critical in helping a client heal because they will learn that it is acceptable to feel fear without always having a flight response (Lustbader, 2019). As a result, the client experiences improvement in daily living and social interactions with peers while reducing overall anxiety and negative thought patterns.

**Program structure.** Exposure therapy can be delivered in a multitude of variations. The American Psychological Association (n.d.) outlines four specific strategies for exposure therapy.

- In vivo exposure – Clients are instructed to directly face fears in real life; for example, a patient who suffers a fear of spiders may be instructed to allow a spider to crawl across their arm. The goal is to have the patient experience the fear, feel it, and learn to cope with it without allowing it to take over.
- Imaginal exposure – Therapists elicit patients to experience vivid recollections of traumatic events or feared objects, situations, or activities. In this way, patients can relive the trauma or fear in a safe environment while learning to work through their negative feelings and thoughts.
- Virtual reality exposure – When in vivo exposure is not practical, virtual reality exposure can take its place. Using virtual reality exposure can help clients to experience fearful experiences within the safety of the therapist's office; for example, patients who are intensely afraid of flying can participate in a flight simulation using virtual reality.
- Interoceptive exposure – This method encourages patients to experience physical sensations that are feared but are actually harmless; for example, patients who fear a rapid heartbeat because they think they are having a heart attack may be instructed to run on a treadmill to learn that a rapid heartbeat is a normal sensation.

Regardless of the exposure strategy, therapists can choose to pace clients differently depending on the severity of fear and level of need. Therapists can gradually expose clients to fear objects, activities, or situations, increasing exposure as clients show a tolerance, or therapists can choose to begin treatment with the most difficult task on the fear hierarchy (American Psychiatric Association, n.d.). Therapists can also practice systemic desensitization, which incorporates exposure and relaxation techniques in order to help the client manage personal experiences more productively.

**Treatment outcomes.** Studies indicate that the results of exposure therapy are promising for alleviating the symptoms of certain disorders. In an analysis of eight studies on narrative exposure therapy and PTSD in survivors of mass violence, McPherson (2012) discovered positive evidence indicating that PTSD symptoms were lessened in this population through the use of the narrative exposure therapy technique. Results of this technique showed better results than a number of other interventions, including supportive counseling, group therapy, and treatment-as-usual.

In a pilot study of individuals suffering from panic disorder, Meuret, Twohig, Rosenfield, Hayes, & Craske (2012) discovered that exposure therapy, coupled with acceptance and commitment therapy, is a likely effective intervention for patients with this disorder. The reduction in symptoms in patients participating in the study was greater than in other CBT trials. Although the sample size was small (11 patients), the likelihood that this study could be replicated with similar results is high, especially given that exposure therapy has a record of effectiveness for anxiety disorders in general (Foa & McLean, 2016; Schare & Wyatt, 2013). While the literature on exposure therapy is not as broad as other forms of CBTs, and future studies are needed to confirm its validity as a stable treatment option, evidence suggests that patients engaging in this form of treatment will find greater improvements over avoidance mechanisms.

## Final Thoughts

While there are many methods of therapy to choose from when considering the individual treatment modality, as with other modalities, care should be taken to choose an intervention that has a high likelihood of success given the patient's characteristics. None of the approaches outlined in this chapter fit all patient needs; for example, exposure therapy may be suitable for some clients with PTSD, but others may benefit from a basic CBT approach. It is also important to remember that not all patients who seek therapy need clinical levels of support (CSUCI, 2019). Keeping this in mind can help practitioners to choose a treatment plan that is most effective for clients with less severe needs. As with all interventions, the goal of therapy is to encourage the patient to be as self-sufficient outside of treatment as possible. Working with clients to develop goals and treatment plans that can be measured is a proven way of helping to prevent relapse in symptoms and to promote healthy replacement behaviors irrespective of client profile.

## Points to Remember

- *Individual therapy is the most widely practiced form of psychotherapy; however, not everyone who seeks treatment is suffering from a severe mental illness.*
- *Four of the most commonly-used EBPs in individual therapy – cognitive behavior therapy, dialectical behavior therapy,*

- *exposure therapy, and mindfulness-based cognitive therapy – are also the most well-studied.*
- *When looking at the likelihood of therapeutic success, several client and therapist characteristics should be considered including client's expectation of treatment, therapist's personality, client's motivation, and ability for the client and therapist to form a positive therapeutic alliance.*
- *Research on the outcomes of EBPs in individual therapy generally show positive results yet, like other forms of therapy, certain therapies work best with specific client profiles and disorders.*
- *As with all interventions, the goal of therapy is to encourage the patient to be as self-sufficient outside of treatment as possible.*

# Chapter Four

# Engaging the Clan: Evidenced-Based Family Therapy Practices

There are many definitions of family, including that which one is born into, that which one is adopted into, and that which one acquires by way of bonds forged in friendship. Some families can be quite healthy, whereas others can be dysfunctional. No matter the type, family affects an individual's behavior and personality as it is often from family that individuals learn how to observe and interact with the world. Families also teach individuals about relationships. Unfortunately, depending on the family structure, these relationships can be strained, creating complex challenges for family members.

While there is no such thing as a perfect family, families that go through periodic dysfunction often can regain their sense of wholeness without the need for therapeutic intervention (Ackerman, 2017). Some families, however, become so broken by traumatic events that they find it difficult to overcome and they require some sort of assistance to help strengthen the interpersonal relationships within the unit.

Traumatic events that affect families can appear in a variety of contexts. One of the most common reasons for family strife occurs when a family member develops a substance abuse disorder (Baldwin, Christian, Berkeljon, & Shadish, 2012). Oftentimes, this disorder has a ripple effect on family dynamics. Once the backbone of the family structure is broken, it is difficult for the unit to retain its support for the affected family member. Unfortunately, children are often the likely victim of strained family dynamics and are more likely to develop substance abuse problems as a result (Filges, Andersen, & Klint-Jorgensen, 2018).

Family therapists are tasked with serving an increasingly difficult-to-treat client group. For families in which there are children with behavioral and substance abuse problems, therapists must treat the individual as well as the family structure (Gehart, 2012). Families who are related by blood may have a history of mental illness, creating more substantial challenges for therapists. In order to effectively promote recovery for both individuals and families, therapists must examine practices that can be used as part of a multi-faceted approach to treatment (Johnson & Wittenborn, 2012; Sexton & Turner, 2011).

There are a variety of EBPs in existence that have shown positive effects on treating dysfunctional family units. Among these, functional family therapy (FFT), emotionally-focused family therapy (EFFT), and brief strategic family therapy (BSFT) are perhaps some of the most widely-used EBPs in family practice. Therapists must consider both the strengths and challenges of each type of therapy, as well as the specific dynamics of the families with whom they work, before choosing which practice would be most appropriate for their clients. There is not a one-size-fits-all approach to family therapy, even for families whose characteristics appear similar.

## Client Characteristics to Consider

While family therapy is a type of treatment designed to target specific issues that plague a family and its ability to function in a healthy manner, not all families respond in similar ways to the same treatment. Some families can face a major transition, such as the death of the family patriarch, with a basic level of treatment; however, there are some families who may face the same loss, yet completely break apart and would be candidates for more intensive intervention. As a result, therapists must consider several different characteristics before determining treatment, such as socioeconomic status, quality of parent-child relationships, quality of communication within the family dynamic, and type of family structure (blended, gay, unmarried, and so forth).

### Socioeconomic Status

As with all types of therapy, socioeconomic status has an impact on treatment outcomes. Counselor perceptions can negatively impact treatment of clients from lower socioeconomic statuses if therapists view these clients as having higher rates of dysfunction, decreased goal-setting for treatment, and an overall less successful outcome than their higher socioeconomic status counterparts (Hawley, Leibert, & Lane, 2017).

Clients who live at or near the poverty line may also be unfairly labeled as lacking motivation for successful treatment, partly due to their oftentimes inconsistent attendance in therapy. Variables such as the cost of treatment, having basic needs met, lack of transportation, and other external stressors are infrequently considered (Hawley et al., 2017). Counselors must work to remove personal biases about the socioeconomic status from the treatment plans. Options that promote self-healing outside of therapy must be considered for these types of clients.

**Quality of Parent-Child Relationships**

In families impacted by children suffering from mental health disorders, it is necessary for therapists to consider the parent-child dynamics, and how these have impacted the child's behavior and development. For children who struggle to adapt to transitions within the family unit, therapists must consider the history of child-rearing and its impact on the child's current presentation (Koolaee, Lor, Soleimani, & Rahmatizadeh, 2014). For many children, disruptions in attachment, authoritarian parenting style, poor supervision, and a lack of healthy role models can all impact the child's behavior and mental health (Hoeve, Dubas, Gerris, van der Laan, & Smeenk, 2011).

These factors can also result in an increased rate of juvenile delinquency down the road. In these cases, therapists must examine the relationship between parent, child, and other family members, to determine how to best treat the behavior that is being exhibited. Additional factors that must be considered in this context would be parental understanding their role, substance abuse disorders, mental health issues, and other socioeconomic factors (Koolaee et al., 2014).

**Quality of Communication**

Many families have difficulties with communication; however, some are more profound than others. For instance, families that consist of cross-generational members, such as children, parents, and grandparents, oftentimes have difficulty with effective communication (Ackerman, 2017). Cultural constraints can impact communication, specifically if one generation of family members does not speak the same language or does not practice the same cultural norms as elder members.

Sometimes communication can impact the relationship between parents and children, especially if there is a disabled child in the family. Siblings may feel as though they are being ignored in favor of the disabled child, and parents may not be sure how to broach the subject with younger children (Wake Forest University, n.d.). A misunderstanding in communication can impact even the best of intentions. Therapists must consider the ways in which the family communicates and subsequently build treatment plans that improve these skills within the entirety of the family structure.

**Family Structure**

As mentioned earlier, families can be a mix of blood relatives, non-relatives, and friends. How family is defined is less important than the way it functions as a support system for the individuals inside the unit. There are many times, however, when the family system is not the problem; rather, it is the societal attitude toward the family structure that causes issues. In families where unmarried or gay couples are raising children, there is often a stigma associated with this type of family unit (Ackerman, 2017). Studies have shown that children from these types of family structures are more likely to suffer from depression than children from traditional families (Altamarino & Chandler, 2013). This is mostly due to the societal pressures put upon children from these families, and a lack of knowledge from parents about how to help their children cope.

Blended families also face struggles, specifically in relation to the adjustment period needed for children. A study by Hetherington & Stanley-Hagan (1995) suggested that children in blended families are 75% more likely to display symptoms of withdrawal, aggressive behavior, and depression than children in traditional households (Altamarino & Chandler, 2013). In order for therapists to treat non-traditional families successfully, care must be taken to consider the family's unique situation and the underlying internal and external stressors influencing their cohesion.

## Evidence-Based Approaches for Families

Because the family dynamics play an important role in the development of problems in children and adolescents, as well as influences the exacerbation of existing mental health conditions among family members, there has been significant interest in family-based interventions, particularly surrounding the ways in which these treatments can help put an end to juvenile delinquency rates among adolescents (Sexton & Turner, 2011). Much of the recent research on family-based therapies focuses on treatment for adolescents with mental health conditions who are likely to experience co-morbid conduct and substance abuse problems (Filges et al., 2018; Sexton & Turner, 2011).

Three of the most widely-used interventions for families - functional family therapy, emotionally-focused family therapy, and brief strategic family therapy – have shown the most promise in helping to ameliorate treatment outcomes for adolescents with substantial mental health disorders (Baldwin et al., 2012; Datchi & Sexton, 2013; Filges et al., 2018; Gehart, 2012; Johnson & Wittenborn, 2012; Lindstrom, Filges, & Klint Jorgensen, 2015; Sexton & Turner, 2011). The focus of these therapies is to integrate the treatment of the individual and family unit through improving family interactions and relationships by reducing dysfunctional behavior of individual family members (Filges et al., 2018; Sexton & Turner, 2011).

### Functional Family Therapy (FFT)

FFT is designed to be a short-term family therapy that is based on a manualized system of delivery (Filges et al., 2018). FFT mainly targets children and adolescents who exhibit problems with substance abuse, juvenile delinquency, and violent tendencies. During the course of the intervention, the therapist attempts to help the family recognize patterns of dysfunctional behavior that are contributing to the young person's problem behavior, and then change those behaviors through improving family dynamics (Sexton & Turner, 2011).

The therapist aims to help the family improve communication, build conflict resolution skills, increase effective problem-solving, and develop better parenting skills (Filges et al., 2018). Once a targeted behavior has been changed within the family, the practitioner helps the family apply that to a variety of other situations and settings outside of the family, such as community and school.

FFT targets the family as a system. The therapist helps the family to recognize its role in the development and treatment of the adolescent's substance abuse and/or conduct disorders. The goal of FFT is not to target one individual patient; rather, to examine the role that the relational dynamics play in fostering these problems. Families are tasked with changing their problematic behaviors, which will, in turn, help to lessen individual behavioral challenges (Datchi & Sexton, 2013; Filges et al., 2018).

In families where hostility runs high, individuals may seek out relationships with outsiders who can fill the void of familial support. Especially in the case of children and adolescents, individuals will engage in negative behaviors in order to gain the attention of family members, regardless of whether the attention is negative (Datchi & Sexton, 2013).

**Program structure.** With the aim of holistically changing the behavior patterns of the family, FFT can help put an end to fractured family systems through deliberate goal-setting and activities. The program is designed so that families attend anywhere from 12 to 20 sessions over the course of three to eight months (Datchi & Sexton, 2013). There are five major components to FFT: engagement, motivation, relational assessment, behavior change, and generalization (Functional Family Therapy, LLC, 2018).

Practitioners first attempt to target aspects of the family unit that create negative interpersonal relationships. To do this, therapists engage in cognitive restructuring and rebuilding alliances within the family (Datchi & Sexton, 2013). Next, therapists focus on building skills within the family as well as relational changes. For family members who lack problem-solving and conflict resolution skills, this part of treatment is crucial in developing the ability to express feelings in a healthy manner. Lastly, practitioners help family members to build up their resiliency in the face of external stressors. They do this by helping families to generalize what they've learned in practice to a wide variety of scenarios in the real world (Datchi & Sexton, 2013).

**Treatment outcomes.** While there is evidence that FFT positively impacts the family dynamic, therefore helping to alleviate the rates of juvenile delinquency and related problems, there are some mixed reviews on its efficacy over treatment-as-usual techniques. In a meta-analysis of studies on FFT effectiveness, Baldwin et al. (2012) discovered that FFT appears to only modestly exceed the effects of treatment-as-usual and other alternate therapies. This review also brought to light the lack of studies that examined which treatments are most effective for families, and on which conditions do family therapies, in general, have the biggest impact.

Similarly, Sexton & Turner (2011) discovered that FFT was no more effective on youth offenders than the supervised probation services model that is most common. The study noted that an important indicator of overall success for FFT is therapist adherence to the program, observing that FFT resulted in a 34.9% reduction in felonies and a 21.1% reduction in misdemeanors as opposed to other treatment options (Sexton & Turner, 2011). As with other interventions, it would appear that fidelity to the program is critical in producing successful outcomes for patients.

It is important to note that although FFT is designed to be primarily used with adolescents who suffer from substance abuse and conduct disorders, FFT can benefit adult offenders as well. Datchi & Sexton (2013) examined whether or not FFT could have an impact on adult criminal conduct. The researchers theorized that utilizing FFT for adult offenders had merit, considering that the goal of FFT is to recognize that family dynamics play a role in offenses, and to change the behaviors within the family to promote more healthy interpersonal interactions, resulting in a stronger support system overall. While more studies are needed in this area to support FFT as a truly effective method of treatment for adult offenders, it seems likely that FFT can have a positive impact on adults who adhere to treatments as part of their rehabilitation.

**Emotionally-Focused Family Therapy (EFFT)**

EFFT differs from other treatment models in that it does not focus on problem-solving within the family unit or examine family histories for the precise timing of breakdowns or the specific family member involved. EFFT instead focuses on increasing family members' abilities to help promote mental health recovery in their loved ones (Johnson & Wittenborn, 2012; Mental Health Foundations, 2018). The therapist's role is to help empower caregivers within the family to support the recovery of the afflicted individual.

EFFT was first developed as a method to help support individuals who suffered from eating disorders; however, EFFT has grown to include general mental health issues, such as depression and anxiety, and the impact on the well-being of the family structure (Ackerman, 2019b). Emotionally-focused therapy is also used in couples' therapy as a method of teaching individuals how to build empathy for each other in the relationship (Johnson & Wittenborn, 2012). EFFT is similar in that it teaches caregivers how to become emotional coaches for their loved ones, specifically with regard to helping them manage stress, cope with negative emotions, and handle life's transition in a productive way (Mental Health Foundations, 2018).

**Program structure.** EFFT operates on the premise of three assumptions. Johnson, Maddeaux, & Blouin (1998) outlined these assumptions over two decades ago and they still form the basis of the program today. The first assumption is that problems in relationships continue due to negative interactions that are encouraged by fear, grief, and anger (Johnson et al., 1998). Internal family drama is exacerbated by these emotions; therefore, narrowing communication and promoting insecurity among family members.

The second assumption suggests that attachment issues are most problematic in developing insecurity within the family; for example, when an individual feels securely attached, they will often turn to this support person for comfort (Johnson et al., 1998). For individuals lacking attachment to family members, negative emotions, such as anxiety, will take over, creating a disconnect between the individual and the family.

The final assumption suggests that emotion is the most critical component in helping to organize attachment behaviors and promoting self-regulation (Johnson et al., 1998).

EFFT consists of three stages of treatment. The treatment is designed to be approximately 10 sessions in length (Johnson et al., 1998).

1. The first stage focuses on de-escalating the family member's negative behaviors or interactions and assists them in understanding what is happening in the relationship. The goal of this stage is to help family members understand that negative behaviors are rooted in personal insecurities that must be acknowledged before healing can occur (Psychology Today, 2018).
2. The second stage focuses on restructuring interactions within the family unit, encouraging family members to look toward each other for support. The goal is to increase family members' responsiveness toward the individual so that there are feelings of value and support.
3. The therapist assists clients to reexamine their negative patterns and take note of how they developed these patterns. At that point, clients can generalize this knowledge into new situations, focusing on behavior modification (Psychology Today, 2018).

**Treatment outcomes.** In a study conducted by Johnson et al. (1998) on individuals suffering from bulimia, results were encouraging as EFFT had a positive impact upon treatment. The results of that study indicated a 52% decrease in bingeing, and a 66.6% overall remission in patients within EFFT treatment as compared to those receiving cognitive behavioral therapy (Johnson et al., 1998). Although this sample is quite small, it highlights the possibility that further studies of EFFT and eating disorders will result in positive treatment outcomes.

More recently, studies have shown that EFFT results in positive outcomes for general mental health conditions. In a study by Foroughe et al. (2018), an examination of parents' ability to play a major role in their child's mental health recovery exhibited positive findings. Out of 124 parents who completed the intervention, the results indicate that parents were able to significantly increase their self-efficacy with regard to helping their children reduce mental health symptomatology (Foroughe et al., 2018).

In a study by Strahan et al. (2017), parents' feelings of fear and self-blame were examined in relation to their child's recovery from an eating disorder. Results indicated that by processing parental feelings and subsequent maladaptive behaviors, parents were more likely to feel empowered and support their child's recovery (Strahan et al., 2017). By targeting the self-efficacy of caregivers and increasing their ability to manage their own feelings, parents were better able to focus on their child's recovery efforts, while being encouraged to become a primary support person for their child (Strahan et al., 2017).

A similar, yet earlier study by Lafrance Robinson, Dolhanty, & Greenberg (2015) supported the notion of caregiver self-efficacy as a means of encouragement in patient recovery. The researchers purported that EFFT was able to assist with a parent's ability to become the child's emotional coach and could help prevent any negative emotional blocks that interfere with the caregiver's ability to support the patient's recovery. These studies support the probability that EFFT is a successful intervention for a range of mental health issues.

**Brief Strategic Family Therapy (BSFT)**

BSFT is a manualized treatment that focuses primarily on adolescent substance abuse. BSFT is problem-focused family therapy that targets making changes in interpersonal interactions influencing negative behaviors in individuals and families who are resistant to change (Lindstrom et al., 2015). BSFT aims to treat adolescents and their families as a system rather than as individual components. Like FFT, BSFT recognizes that the family plays a critical role in the development of substance abuse in adolescents.

Developed in the early 1970s as a treatment method for addressing the cultural needs of the Hispanic population in Miami who demonstrated substance abuse and behavioral disorders, BSFT has since been adapted to serve other populations, specifically other groups who need a culturally-sensitive treatment option (Lindstrom et al., 2015; Robbins & Szapocznik, 2000). Based on family systems theory, BFST focuses on understanding an individual's behavior in relation to the family context. Problem behavior in young people is generally seen as being associated with negative social interaction patterns within the family structure, so in order to stop problem behaviors, patterns of negative interaction within the family must be targeted and addressed before individual recovery is possible (Lindstrom et al., 2015).

**Program structure.** There are three major components to BSFT treatment: joining, diagnosing, and restructuring. Joining refer to the process of engaging the individual and family in treatment by establishing a solid therapeutic relationship (Lindstrom et al., 2015). The therapist aims to build an alliance with both the individual members and the family as a whole, essentially becoming a temporary family member (Robbins & Szapocznik, 2000).

Next, the therapist focuses on identifying problematic behaviors and interactions within the family, called the diagnosing stage. In order to accomplish this, therapists must create a way for family members to interact within their typical style. The therapist then observes the pattern of inappropriate interactions and relationship within the family structure. Discovering and diagnosing these negative aspects of familial interaction help the therapist to determine the ways in which the family struggles with helping to reduce the adolescent's substance abuse problems (Lindstrom et al., 2015).

The goal of the final component – restructuring – focuses on changing the maladaptive behaviors of the family that are related to the adolescent's drug use and turn them into more successful ways of interacting (Robbins & Szapocznik, 2000). Components of the restructuring phase include working in the present, reframing, and working with boundaries and alliances.

Treatment components can be tailored based on the individual and family needs and focus on the likelihood that the patient will either recover or relapse. The program is designed to consist of approximately 12-16 sessions, yet that number can be adjusted depending on the needs of the clients. BSFT is also flexible in that it can be performed in a wide variety of settings, including clinical and community facilities, or in the family home (Lindstrom et al., 2015).

**Treatment outcomes.** Unfortunately, although BSFT is a widely-accepted and practiced EBP, there is limited statistical evidence on its overall effectiveness. Lindstrom et al. (2015) performed a meta-analysis on studies of BSFT effectiveness, specifically on substance abusing adolescents. The researchers discovered that with regard to abstinence or reduction or drug use, the studies examined did not indicate a statistically significant effect from BSFT treatment. This finding suggests that BSFT and other types of interventions likely have similar outcomes when compared.

With regard to family functioning, examined studies once again did not indicate a statistically significant improvement at the end of treatment with BSFT (Lindstrom et al., 2015). This finding suggests that community treatment programs and other forms of treatment are likely as effective as BSFT at increasing family functioning at the end of treatment. Conversely, for treatment retention, BSFT has shown a greater impact than treatment-as-usual techniques; however, the number of studies examined for these analyses are relatively small, so conclusions regarding the long-term efficacy of BSFT cannot be generalized (Lindstrom et al., 2015). It is clear that more studies are needed to determine whether or not a statistically significant improvement in treatment outcomes is likely.

## Final Thoughts

EBPs in family practice are quickly becoming the default method for treating families who suffer from internal dysfunction, as well as for addressing individual family members who suffer from conditions such as eating or substance abuse disorders. In general, EBP studies suggest positive treatment outcomes for families who engage in these interventions. More studies are needed to confirm their effectiveness across contexts and with a variety of mental health disorders. As with other treatment modalities, the most successful families are those whose therapist adheres closely to treatment protocol, while remaining flexible enough to tailor the program to meet the individual needs of the family.

## Points to Remember

- *Family affects an individual's behavior and personality as it is often from family that individuals learn how to observe and interact with the world.*
- *For families in which there are children with behavioral and substance abuse problems, therapists must treat the individual as well as the family structure.*
- *Therapists must consider several different characteristics before determining treatment, such as socioeconomic status, quality of parent-child relationships, quality of communication within the family dynamic, and type of family structure (blended, gay, unmarried, etc.).*
- *The focus of using EBPs for families is to integrate the treatment of the individual and family unit through improving family interactions and relationships by reducing dysfunctional behavior of individual family members.*
- *While there are some studies showing the effectiveness of FFT, EFFT, and BSFT in treatment outcomes, more research is needed to support this conclusion.*

# Chapter Five

# Expanding the Support System: Evidenced-Based Group Therapy Practices

Group therapy is a relatively recently accepted, widely practiced method of working with patients. Prior to World War II, there were only a few physicians that practiced group therapy in favor of the more traditional emphasis of the development of the doctor-patient relationship (Barlow, Fuhriman, & Burlingame, 2004). As soldiers returned from the war, it was evident that there would be an overwhelming need for mental health services. Group therapy was born of this need, wherein psychiatrists would treat soldiers in groups to maximize the services that one psychiatrist could provide (Barlow, Fuhriman, & Burlingame, 2004). As this practice advanced, it was clear that group therapy was an effective method for treating individuals who had similar challenges.

Today, group therapy has grown to include treatment options for everything from eating disorders to social anxiety and substance abuse. Although the benefits of group therapy can be promising, therapists who choose this modality must be aware that this type of therapy has its limitations (American Psychiatric Association, 2019a). Therapists who choose group therapy instead of individual therapy for specific client profiles must consider the characteristics of the group in order to determine the likelihood of treatment success (Hunnicutt Hollenbaugh, 2011).

An analysis of 125 studies discovered that group treatment dropout rates were approximately 47% (Wierzbicki & Pekarik, 1993). Recent analyses have shown similar results (Swift & Greenberg, 2012). In one analysis, over 699 studies were reviewed, and the results indicated that although more clients remained in group therapy, the dropout rate is approximately 1 in 5. Studies also indicate that the increasing use of evidence-based practices in group therapy can have an impact not only on client retention, but also on the long-term effectiveness of treatment, even for group members who do not follow the program to completion (Ghee, Bolling, & Johnson, 2009; Hien et al., 2011).

## Client Characteristics to Consider

It is necessary to consider several characteristics of clients in order to determine who is likely to be a successful candidate for this type of intervention. When examining client demographics, factors such as age, education, socioeconomic status, diagnosis, and treatment expectations can all have substantial impacts on the outcome of treatment.

### Age

Studies show that age can be a predicting factor in the success rate of group therapy (Hunnicutt Hollenbaugh, 2011). The younger the client, the more likely they are to drop out of treatment or, at the very least, decide not to follow through with all treatment stages.

### Education and Socioeconomic Status

Individuals who have lower levels of education are less likely to follow through with group treatment. Level of education oftentimes correlates with socioeconomic status; therefore, studies suggest that individuals who have a high school diploma or who have dropped out of school, along with income in or around the poverty level, are less likely to continue participating in group treatment (Hebert & Bergeron, 2007).

### Diagnosis

While group therapy may be effective for a multitude of diagnoses, there are a few that remain challenging for group therapy treatment; specifically, substance abuse disorders, antisocial personality disorder, and borderline personality disorder have been cited as the most difficult disorders to experience successful treatment through the group therapy method (Hunnicutt Hollenbaugh, 2011). Substance abuse disorders often occur simultaneously with trauma-related disorders, and it can often be difficult to treat both with the same level of efficacy (Hien et al., 2012).

Studies show that substance abuse disorders are a major factor in group therapy dropout rates due to the likelihood of relapse (Witkiewitz & Bowen, 2010). There are some programs that have shown promise in reducing the number of dropouts, as well as strengthening the outcome of treatment in those individuals who have left therapy before program completion; however, these factors are dependent upon the individual patient (Patitz et al., 2015).

Another diagnosis that is difficult to effectively treat in group therapy is borderline personality disorder (BPD). Patients who are diagnosed with this disorder can be especially difficult to treat due to the nature of the disorder which is characterized by impairments in empathy, intimacy, self-direction, and self-image, as well as emotional liability, anxiety, and separation insecurity (American Psychiatric Association, 2013). In patients with BPD, higher levels of aggression, impulsivity, and manipulation have been reported as being present during group therapy (Gunderson et al., 2006; Hunnicutt Hollenbaugh, 2011).

Similar to BPD, antisocial personality disorder can be extremely difficult to treat in a group setting. Like BPD, patients who are diagnosed with antisocial personality disorder are characterized by a lack of empathy, difficulties with intimate relationships, and impairments in self-functioning. However, clients with this disorder often experience hostility toward others, deceitfulness, and risk-taking behavior (American Psychiatric Association, 2013). This can make it extremely challenging to work with these individuals within the group setting. Even if treatment is marginally successful for patients with antisocial personality disorder (as well as other disorders), the ever-changing nature of some group therapy sessions can prove to be detrimental to treatment efficacy (Morgan-Lopez, Saavedra, Hien, & Fals-Stewart, 2011).

**Treatment Expectations**

For patients who have not completely bought into the idea of group therapy, treatment can have varied effects. Studies have suggested that a patient's attitude toward treatment and the belief that the modality can be successful has a substantial impact on whether or not the treatment is indeed successful (Hunnicutt Hollenbaugh, 2011; Kuusisto, Knuuttila, & Saarnio, 2011). Similarly, for patients who felt that the therapist's role was the most important in determining success of treatment, the percentage of success rates was higher than in individuals who felt they could discontinue therapy without completion and still be successful (Kuusisto, Knuuttila, & Saarnio, 2011).

While this is not an exhaustive list of client characteristics to consider, it is important to examine the client's full profile when determining the likelihood of success with the group therapy method. It is also necessary to note that the above-mentioned traits may not have a negative impact in group therapy for certain individuals. It is best to consider each client individually when determining their fitness for this modality.

## Evidence-Based Approaches for Groups

In recent years, there have been a number of studies examining the effectiveness of evidence-based practices in group settings, specifically with patients who have experienced trauma and/or substance abuse. Two of the more popular approaches, Seeking Safety and mindfulness-based relapse prevention (MBRP), have garnered much attention due to their effectiveness with patients who have similar disorders but have mixed backgrounds (Hien et al., 2012). These two practices share a common theme of flexibility, allowing for patients to gain the skills necessary to practice the tenets of treatment outside of direct treatment times (Ghee, Bolling, & Johnson, 2009; Witkiewitz & Bowen, 2010).

**Seeking Safety**

For patients who are battling trauma and/or substance abuse, the Seeking Safety program can be used to help mitigate the psychological symptoms associated with trauma and, in turn, help lessen the chance of substance abuse relapse in patients who use drugs and alcohol as a means of coping (Ghee et al., 2009). Seeking Safety is an evidence-based program grounded in cognitive behavior therapy that focuses on using coping skills to deal with both trauma and substance abuse (Ghee et al., 2009; Treatment Innovations, 2016).

The program was developed in 1992 and has been widely used across the globe to help with concomitant substance abuse and trauma disorders. As many individuals who suffer from trauma utilize drugs and alcohol to help numb the painful memories of their experiences, Seeking Safety aims to teach participants about safe coping mechanisms so that they can work through their trauma productively (Patitz et al., 2015).

**Program structure.** Seeking Safety includes 25 treatment topics that are used over just as many sessions in order to integrate trauma and substance abuse intervention (Ghee et al., 2009). The following is an overview of the Seeking Safety treatment topics adapted from the program manual (Treatment Innovations, 2016).

1. Introduction to treatment – getting to know the patient and assessing the patient's individual needs.

2. Safety – Counselors describe safety as the first stage of healing from trauma and substance abuse. Counselors provide patients with a list of safe coping skills, and patients can evaluate their own definitions of safety and how that definition can have a positive impact on treatment.
3. PTSD: Taking Back Your Power – Understanding PTSD and its link to substance abuse is explored in this session. The counselor's goal is to provide clients with an understanding of PTSD and provide a way of compassionately working with the disorder.
4. Detaching from Emotional Pain: Grounding – Patients are introduced to grounding as a method of detaching from the emotions associated with trauma. In this session, the goal is to teach clients ways in which to focus on the external world instead of internalizing their emotions.
5. When Substances Control You – The goal of this session is to have clients recognize the characteristics of substance abuse disorders and to admit that they have a problem, as well as to have clients engage in scenarios where they prepare to give up their substance reliance.
6. Asking for Help – Because trauma and substance abuse disorders can impair patients when it comes to seeking help, this session encourages patients to become aware of their need for assistance and determine the best methods for obtaining it.
7. Taking Good Care of Yourself – Clients are asked to reflect upon how well they are taking care of themselves. For instance, a questionnaire asks the patient to provide answers to questions about such topics as how often they get regular medical check-ups. After completing this questionnaire, patients are encouraged to take action to improve at least one aspect of their self-care.
8. Compassion – Instead of berating oneself over perceived guilt with regard to trauma and substance abuse, the goal of this session is to provide patients with an understanding of compassion and the way in which to use it toward oneself. Patients are encouraged to be loving and accepting of themselves as a method of healing.
9. Red and Green Flags – This session focuses on helping patients develop a safety plan when it comes to factors that can impede treatment. Red and green flags are used as a

metaphor for danger and safety. Patients are taught what to do in situations that may make them feel unsafe.
10. Honesty – Counselors help patients to understand the role of honesty, both with oneself and with others. Specifically, clients are helped to understand when honesty is a safe option, and what to do when the other person is unaccepting of the client's honesty.
11. Recovery Thinking – Counselors encourage patients to rethink their options with alternate outcomes. Patients are challenged with creating a new story for themselves, as well as to challenge their old ways of thinking.
12. Integrating the Split Self – Because both PTSD and substance abuse can create dual sides of the self as a means of coping, it is necessary for clients to understand the signs of separation and to work to integrate these sides into one; for instance, denial as a coping mechanism does not allow for the work to begin on accepting the trauma and moving forward.
13. Commitment – Clients are encouraged to work on making promises and commitments and keeping them. Counselors also work on helping patients understand and work through feelings that may get in the way of following through with commitments.
14. Creating Meaning – Clients are encouraged to understand the meaning behind their actions and to recognize harmful versus healing practices.
15. Community Resources – Clients are provided with lists of community resources that can help with recovery. Counselors help patients to self-evaluate treatment options so that they can continue to choose interventions that are beneficial to their recovery.
16. Setting Boundaries in Relationships – Oftentimes, boundary awareness is difficult for patients, specifically for those who have experienced physical and emotional abuse. Counselors aim to help clients recognize healthy boundaries and work to help them create such a system in their own lives.
17. Discovery – In this session, clients are encouraged to remain open to new experiences and to break free from rigid thinking patterns. Counselors also help clients to handle negative responses from others.
18. Getting Others to Support Your Recovery – Clients are encouraged to identify individuals in their lives who will be supportive of their recovery efforts. Counselors provide

assistance with learning how to gain support from individuals, as well as effective and safe ways to spread awareness about their disorder to these chosen individuals.
19. Coping with Triggers – Because relapse is common for individuals who suffer from both trauma and substance abuse, it is necessary to teach patients the tools necessary to avoid situations that may trigger them into reaching for a substance. Specifically, the program provides a three-step model: change who you are with, what you are doing, and where you are. This model is designed to remove the patient from the triggering situation and potentially locate a supportive person to help break the cycle of relapse.
20. Respecting Your Time – An unfortunate side effect of trauma/substance abuse disorders is the amount of time lost in one's life. Although patients may have been emotionally absent from their lives for years, they can look forward to developing new plans for the future. Counselors help patients to work on making plans and prioritizing their lives.
21. Healthy Relationships – Counselors challenge patient thinking about what constitutes a good or bad relationship. In this session, counselors focus on helping patients build skills that will assist in developing positive relationships. They also focus on teaching patients the ways in which their disorders can lead to the development of negative relationships.
22. Self-Nurturing – In this session, counselors help patients to recognize unsafe practices of self-nurturing, such as using substances to cope, versus safe practices that help the patient to develop a healthy sense of self.
23. Healing from Anger – As many patients are dealing with anger as a side effect from trauma, it is necessary to help them work through anger in a constructive way. Because anger can be used both positively and negatively, patients are taught how to channel their anger into self-improving behaviors versus relapse.
24. The Life Choices Game – This is the last step before program termination, and it takes all of the teachings throughout the program and puts them into a culminating experience. Patients select challenging real-life scenarios from a box and discuss how they would cope with these scenarios using the constructive coping mechanisms they've learned throughout the program.

25. Termination – At the final session of the program, patients are encouraged to express their emotions about ending the program, as well as what they liked or disliked during treatment.

**Treatment outcomes.** As previously discussed, not all patients with similar profiles respond in the same ways to specific modalities and the same holds true for this program. Most of the studies involving the outcomes of the Seeking Safety program focus on women, so the effects on men within the program are not well-known. There have been limited studies examining the effects of Seeking Safety on specific subgroups of women; for instance, the ways in which the program impacts women from rural areas who lack access to myriad additional supports has not been overly studied (Patitz et al., 2015; Swift, Callahan, & Levine, 2009).

From the relatively limited number of studies conducted, it is clear that there are benefits for clients who both follow the program to completion and those who attend inconsistently.

Because women with co-occurring trauma and substance abuse disorders often attend sessions of treatment sporadically, it is necessary for therapists to recognize that treatment can oftentimes have a more substantial impact on this group than on women who attend all sessions (Hien et al., 2012).

Although Seeking Safety is designed to have 25 sessions in total, treatment effectiveness has been demonstrated when women attend as few as six sessions (Ghee et al., 2009; Najavits, 2002). One study concluded that, for some women in treatment, a condensed version of the program might be effective due to the barriers that block traditional participation in the program, such as child care, cost, and other family responsibilities (Ghee et al., 2009).

The study conducted by Hien et al. (2012), demonstrated that women who attended inconsistently showed positive outcomes in the reduction of substance use when using the Seeking Safety program. Although their outcomes were not better than program completers in all instances, they were significantly better than participants who quit the program altogether.

In the case of women from rural populations who participate in the program, there is evidence that treatment outcomes can be improved despite this population's unique set of barriers (Patitz et al., 2015). Women who live in rural areas generally have less access to providers and affordable treatment options, as well as facing more stigma within their small communities for seeking assistance (Patitz et al., 2015).

In their pilot study on the topic, Patitz et al. (2015) discovered that participants from rural areas showed a decrease in trauma symptoms from pre- to post-intervention. There is a relative lack of mental health providers in these areas; therefore, therapists who wish to reach a greater number of patients may consider utilizing Seeking Safety in a group setting to increase treatment outcomes for this largely underrepresented subgroup of women.

**Mindfulness-Based Relapse Prevention**

Mindfulness-based relapse prevention (MBRP) is a recently-developed intervention based on the Marlatt and Gordon model of cognitive behavioral relapse prevention (Curry, Marlatt, & Gordon, 1987; Witkiewitz & Bowen, 2010). The model suggests that as a patient is presented with a high-risk situation, there is either a high or low probability of relapse, depending on the individual's coping abilities (Larimer, Palmer, & Marlatt, 1999).

For patients who have effective coping strategies, there is confidence that they can overcome the stressors of the situation and will not fall into relapse (Witkiewitz & Bowen, 2010). For patients who have underdeveloped coping mechanisms, there is a high probability that they will feel overwhelmed by the situation and will turn to substance abuse as a method of coping, which will in turn become the patient's method of choice for coping, ultimately becoming a full-fledged relapse (Witkiewitz & Bowen, 2010).

This model, when coupled with mindfulness training, directly targets a patient's cravings associated with soothing negative emotions by teaching them to observe their emotional, physical, and cognitive experiences at the moment (Witkiewicz & Bowen, 2010).

**Program structure.** MBRP was designed at the University of Washington Addictive Behaviors Research Center and the original research team worked under the mentorship of Dr. Alan Marlatt, on whose cognitive-behavioral relapse prevention model MBRP is based (Bowen, Chawla, & Marlatt, 2010). The goals of MBRP include

- helping patients develop an awareness of personal triggers and the subsequent reactions that come along with them,
- learning ways to stop the automatic response mechanisms,
- changing patients' relationship to discomfort and the ways in which the patient responds,

- becoming more non-judgmental of experiences and develop compassion toward oneself and;
- building a lifestyle that is conducive to healing and preventing relapse (Bowen et al., 2010).

MBRP can be practiced in a multitude of settings; however, as a group therapy practice, MBRP appears to show promising results for lessening the likelihood of relapse among participants in comparison to patients involved in standard treatment such as medication, individual talk therapy, and others (Bowen et al., 2010). MBRP operates on the premise that when a triggering situation occurs, the patient experiences an initial reaction, whether that be thoughts, emotions, or physical sensations (Bowen et al., 2010).

A patient who responds automatically without mindfulness will often believe their thoughts and emotions, lapse into negative behavior, and continue to perseverate on thoughts and emotions. This creates a cycle of relapse from which the patient has difficulty escaping; conversely, when a patient practices mindfulness, they experience an initial reaction, but stop and observe the reaction as well as the feelings associated with it (Abrams & Penn, n.d.). The goal is to observe the reaction without judgment, recognizing that feelings are fleeting. After observing and analyzing the situation, the patient can respond to it with awareness (Teasdale, Segal, & Williams, 1995).

Many institutions offer MBRP training for therapists interested in exploring its effectiveness as a treatment option. The founders of MBRP offer professional training workshops for therapists interested in developing their skill in this intervention (Abrams & Penn, n.d.; Bowen et al., 2010).

**Treatment outcomes.** Because trauma and substance abuse disorders are becoming more prevalent, it is necessary for practitioners to examine a variety of ways in which to treat individuals that will lessen the risk of relapse. Results of relapse based on medication therapy alone are often higher, specifically if the patients stop taking their medication either of their own volition or because they cannot afford it. MBRP provides promising evidence for patients who learn the practice of mindfulness and use it to specifically address depressive symptoms and the cravings for substances that often co-occur (Witkiewicz & Bowen, 2010).

In comparison to some interventions MBRP is relatively new, and so more studies must be conducted to prove its efficacy; however, in studies that have been completed examining its effectiveness with specific subgroups of patients, MBRP has shown positive results. For example, MBRP has been shown to produce positive results in the area of behavior modification for individuals with intellectual disabilities (Harper, Webb, & Rayner, 2013).

For patients with trauma and substance abuse disorders, MBRP has demonstrated the ability to counteract the symptoms of depression, which in turn, often lead to substance abuse relapse (Witkiewicz & Bowen, 2010). There is also evidence suggesting that MBRP alters brain functioning in individuals with depressive symptoms and substance cravings, which is tremendous news for therapists who are looking for treatment options that do not include medication for vulnerable patients (Lutz, Brefczynski-Lewis, Johnsone, & Davidson, 2008).

## Final Thoughts

Group therapy has shown promise as a positive therapy for specific groups of individuals. Many studies have shown that a patient's success rate has more to do with their personal profile than on consistent participation in treatment (Ghee et al., 2009; Hien et al., 2012; Hunnicutt Hollenbaugh, 2011). Patients who inconsistently attend group treatment sessions can increase their success rate in recovery as long as they are willing to practice what they've learned with regard to coping mechanisms and healthy thought processes. This is especially true for patients who attend group therapy sessions where evidence-based practices are used.

Although relatively new, programs such as Seeking Safety and MBRP have shown positive outcomes in studied groups (Bowen et al., 2010; Ghee et al., 2009). Studies have shown that both Seeking Safety and MBRP promote patients' abilities to develop self-calming mechanisms to deal with the side effects of trauma and substance abuse disorders (Patitz et al., 2015; Witkiewicz & Bowen, 2010). Future studies of these and other evidence-based group therapy practices will likely show the efficacy of these types of programs on a multitude of patient subgroups.

## Points to Remember

- *Group therapy is used to treat a variety of disorders, including social anxiety, eating disorders, and substance abuse/trauma.*
- *It is necessary for therapists to consider the patient's profile before assigning them to group therapy. Factors such as age, socioeconomic status, education, and disorder should all be considered when determining the best treatment option.*

- *Evidence-based approaches such as Seeking Safety and mindfulness-based relapse prevention have been widely used to treat patients with substance abuse and trauma disorders.*
- *Both Seeking Safety and MBRP have shown positive treatment outcomes for patients, even for patients who attend sessions inconsistently.*

# Chapter Six

# When it Takes Two to Make a Personal Life Work: Evidenced-Based Couples Therapy Practices

Experts in the therapeutic field believe that therapy is an important part of a couple's relationship and that couples should seek therapy well before they believe it is needed. Couples therapy will give partners the tools and techniques needed to improve conflict resolution and keep small issues from growing in size (Kerner, 2018). Couples should view therapy not as a solution to a crisis, but as an integral part of a healthy relationship, a safe space to discuss sensitive topics, and as a place to learn how to effectively communicate with each other, particularly during times of major life change and transition (Kerner, 2018).

Couples therapy is a type of psychotherapy in which a clinically experienced therapist works with two people involved in a romantic relationship to help them gain insight into their relationship, resolve conflict, and improve relationship satisfaction (Colangelo, 2015). While there are a variety of practices that are used by therapists in couples counseling, most couples therapy involves (1) focusing on a specific problem; (2) active participation by the therapist in treating the relationship itself, not the individuals; (3) solution-focused, change-oriented interventions; and (4) a clear establishment of treatment objectives (Colangelo, 2015).

## Attachment-Based Therapy

Research demonstrates that the origins of couples therapy and some scientific-based therapeutic practices, such as attachment-based therapy, emotionally-focused therapy, and the Gottman method, began with the basis of attachment theory, which states that individuals need a safe relationship in which they can turn to when life becomes too much (Johnson, 2019; Dashnaw, 2017). Secure and close connections with others, shaped by mutual emotional accessibility and responsiveness, can be a source of strength and personality integration, giving securely connected individuals a more articulated and positive sense of self (Johnson, 2019).

Attachment theory examines how individuals' early relationships with a primary caregiver create the expectation for how love and relationships should be (Feuerman, 2019). The attachment style that an individual brings into a relationship, whether it be secure, anxious, dismissive, or disorganized, will often dictate how an individual acts and interacts in a relationship and (Feuerman, 2019).

**Secure Attachment**

Individuals that are securely attached as adults grew up with parents who made them feel safe and loved, met their needs, displayed generous amounts of attention, and were reliably responsive and empathetic (Dashnaw, 2019; Feuerman, 2019). As a result, these individuals tend to be more empathetic, less aggressive, more responsible and reliable, understand themselves and others better, and exude a calm self-possession, thus creating a healthy template for intimate relationships (Dashnaw, 2019; Feuerman, 2019). Individuals that grew up with unresponsive parents are more likely to form an insecure attachment pattern which can manifest itself in one of the main three ways (Feuerman, 2019).

**Anxious/ preoccupied attachment.** For these adults, they grew up with parents that were inconsistent with attention, occasionally reliable, and inconsistent and poor in meeting their child's needs (Dashnaw, 2019; Feuerman, 2019). As a result, partners with anxious attachment can be clingy and demanding in relationships and are unable to foster a sense of calmness within themselves and trust their partner, even with a partner that is reliable and securely attached (Dashnaw, 2019; Feuerman, 2019). Perpetual anxiety can also make these individuals crave intimacy from their relationship partner while simultaneously doubting their own value as a partner and accept that they are loved (Dashnaw, 2019).

**Dismissive/ fearful avoidant attachment.** Adults that display a dismissive, fearful or avoidant type of attachment were raised by parents who met their physical needs but were neglectful as a lifestyle. These individuals were often left to entertain themselves and had no meaningful interactions with their parents, often feeling like their needs would never be met so they should take care of themselves (Dashnaw, 2019; Feuerman, 2019). As adults, these feelings translate into ones that make getting close to another individual scary, of feeling constantly let down, and the dismissal of intimate bonds, often preferring to be alone and independent rather than with others (Dashnaw, 2019; Feuerman, 2019).

**Disorganized attachment.** Disorganized attachment can develop from abuse, trauma, or chaos in a child's home, leaving the child fearing a parent and eliminating their ability to develop a sense of safety or security with intimate others (Dashnaw, 2019; Feuerman, 2019). As adults, these individuals typically have chaotic relationships filled with turmoil, lean on others to manage their feelings, have difficulty asking for help and showing vulnerability, and continuously struggle in relationships. They see people as not only unreliable, but dangerous, which can result in the triggering of traumatic memories, even when parenting their own children (Dashnaw, 2019).

## Couples Therapy

From an attachment perspective, the negative spirals that distressed couples create and feel victimized by as a result of their attachment style are characterized by separation distress and the emotional starvation that results from emotional disconnection (Johnson, 2019). When an individual in an intimate relationship cannot get their partner, or attachment figure, to respond, they begin a hard-wired sequence of hopeful and then angry protest that then turns desperate and coercive, leaving the individual seeking any and all attention (Johnson, 2019).

Attachment-based therapists help partners in distress listen to their emotions, clearly speak their needs, and reach for their partner in a way that will aid their partner in responding. Creating these safe emotional connections can assist each partner positively cope with stress and distress from within and outside the relationship itself (Johnson, 2019). When attachment therapists help partners tune in emotionally to each other, their relationship is able to reach a safe physical and emotional balance that promotes optimal performance (Johnson, 2019).

## Gottman Method

The Gottman Method and The Sound Relationship House Theory were built upon scientific research that examined patterns in observational data among more than 3000 couples that distinguished there were indeed patterns of behavior, or sequences of interactions, that could discriminate happy from unhappy couples (Gottman, 2015).

The resultant theory and method of therapy is now used with couples of all types and can be applied at any stage of life to educate committed partners and restore healthy functioning to distressed couples, whether they are stuck in chronic conflict, coping with infidelity, or engaging in destructive patterns (Moelbak, 2014; Wiebe & Johnson, 2016). During therapy, partners discover their patterns of interaction and learn and implement relationship-building and problem-solving skills together (The Gottman Institute, 2019).

Research shows that negativity can make a tremendous impact on the brain and that unless couples take steps to counteract occurrences of negativity, they will grow emotionally distant (Wiebe & Johnson, 2016). The Gottman Method is used to gain a deeper insight into why partners create the relationship dynamics they do while identifying and addressing the states of mind and behaviors that can underlie intimacy and help partners maintain a positive orientation to each other (The Gottman Institute, 2019). Relationship areas that are commonly addressed include (1) frequent conflict and arguments; (2) poor communication; (3) emotionally distanced couples on the verge of separation; and (4) specific problems such as sexual difficulties, infidelity, money, and parenting (Lewis, 2018; The Gottman Institute, 2019).

Using the Gottman Method approach to couples therapy includes a thorough assessment of a couple's relationship, including a discussion on topics on which the partners disagree, using a conjoint session, individual interviews, and questionnaires to provide detailed feedback on the relationship (Lewis, 2018; The Gottman Institute, 2019).

Therapeutic interventions are then created to assist couples in strengthening their relationships in the areas of friendship, conflict management, and the creation of shared meaning with the goals of disarming conflicting verbal communication, increasing intimacy, respect, and affection, removing barriers, and creating a heightened sense of empathy and understanding within the context of the relationship (Lewis, 2018; The Gottman Institute, 2019).

During therapy sessions, couples learn to replace negative conflict patterns with new approaches to communication and positive interactions as well as repair their past hurts. The couples shared goals are also enhanced through specific interventions that increase closeness and intimacy, improve friendship, and deepen emotional connections (Lewis, 2018; The Gottman Institute, 2019).

### The Sound Relationship House Theory

According to the Gottman Method, key behaviors, known as the four horsemen of the apocalypse, can make a difference in whether a relationship is successful or comes to an end. Behaviors that do not contribute to a healthy, long-lasting relationship include (1) criticism or complaining about a partner and attributing problems in the relationship to some defect in them; (2) defensiveness - not hearing or considering a partner's feedback and not taking ownership or responsibility; (3) stonewalling or mentally withdrawing from a conversation; and (4) showing contempt or displaying disgust towards a partner and/or putting them down (Lewis, 2018; The Gottman Institute, 2019).

In comparison, relationships that are healthy and lead to more relationship satisfaction are built within the context of The Sound Relationship House Theory, comprised of nine research-based interventions (Lewis, 2018; Moelbak, 2014; The Gottman Institute, 2019). The lowest level of the house begins with building love maps. This intervention seeks to discover how well one partner knows the other's inner psychological world, history, worries, stresses, joys, and hopes (Lewis, 2018; The Gottman Institute, 2019). The goal at this level is for each person to develop a clear and accurate knowledge about the other and allocate a room in their mind to truly learn who they are (Moelbak, 2014).

The next level of the relationship house focuses on sharing positive thoughts and feelings within a relationship and has partners express their appreciation and respect for one another to strengthen fondness and admiration (Lewis, 2018; Moelbak, 2014). The next level up has partners state their needs and consciously look for attempts their partner is making to connect and turn towards them (The Gottman Institute, 2019). These micro interactions are engaged in when partners drop what they are doing to respond to something the other is interested in and are moments of interaction and connection that may seem minor but become important when couples grow distant (Moelbak, 2014).

The fourth and fifth levels focus on positive approaches to problem-solving, managing conflict, rather than resolving conflict, and repair attempts made by each partner. Couples are reminded that conflict is natural in a relationship and can even be healthy when it is handled in a positive way (Lewis, 2018; The Gottman Institute, 2019). Maintaining positivity will also enable couples to create an atmosphere that encourages each partner to honestly discuss their hopes, values, convictions and aspirations; thus creating a sense of shared meaning and allow for the understanding of important visions, narratives, myths, and metaphors about the relationship, the next two levels in the relationship house (Lewis, 2018; The Gottman Institute, 2019).

At the uppermost levels of the sound relationship house are trust and commitment, the fundamental building blocks for relationships to even exist (Lewis, 2018; Moelbak, 2014). Trust occurs when an individual in the relationship knows that their partner acts and thinks in a way that will maximize their best interests and benefits and that they are truly there for them. Commitment is not only a belief, but an action upon that belief, that the relationship with your partner is a lifelong journey and in times of difficulty, both individuals will work together to improve the relationship. Instead of enlarging negative qualities and nurturing resentment, partners will cherish each other's positive qualities and nurture gratitude (The Gottman Institute, 2019).

**Emotionally Focused Couples Therapy**

Emotionally focused couples' therapy (EFT) is an empirically validated and structured approach to couples therapy that is used with distressed couples including partners that suffer from disorders such as depression, post-traumatic stress disorders, and chronic illness (Johnson, 2008). Research demonstrates that when involved with EFT, 70-75% of couples move from distress to recovery and approximately 90% show significant improvements (Johnson, 2008).

EFT is an attachment-based approach that is built on clear, explicit conceptualizations of marital distress, adult love, and adult attachment (Johnson, 2004). The distress that partners can feel in a relationship is often related to deeply rooted fears of abandonment and a partner's emotional response to these fears can be harmful and put a strain on their relationship (Good Therapy, 2018). EFT also considers the key principle in couples' conflict to be the insecurity in the attachment one partner has with the other and helps them address this insecurity by teaching them to interact in more loving, responsive, and emotionally connected ways (Good Therapy, 2018).

Using scientifically validated theories of adult bonding and techniques from person-centered therapy, specific change strategies and interventions are used to expand and reorganize key emotional responses, such as fear of abandonment, create a shift in partners' interactional positions, initiate new cycles of interaction, and foster the creation of a secure bond between partners (Johnson, 2008; 2019; Good Therapy, 2018).

Problems within a relationship are one of the main reasons couples seek therapy and studies have shown that the quality of intimate bonds is linked to an individual's mental and physical health outcomes (Johnson, 2019). Loneliness and relationship distress are both risk factors associated with mental health issues such as depression, anxiety, post-traumatic distress and substance addiction. Research studies have also shown that EFT cannot only help couples alleviate relationship distress, improve their relationships, access an optimal level of resilience, but also help alleviate individual co-morbidities as well (Johnson, 2019).

Goals of EFT include helping partners de-escalate negative cycles of interaction, such as angry, critical demanding followed by defensive stonewalling and distance, and move partners into a restructuring process of bonding interactions where they can co-regulate fears of rejection and abandonment, and communicate attachment needs that will invite partner responsiveness (Johnson, 2019; Good Therapy, 2018).

**Phases of Emotionally Focused Therapy.** Emotionally focused therapy involves nine treatment steps and in the initial sessions of treatment couples' interaction styles will be assessed to help de-escalate the conflict. The goal during this period of assess and de-escalate is to uncover the underlying emotional problem and begin to change the way it is perceived by the couple (Good Therapy, 2018; Ackerman, 2017). During stage one, therapists will identify key issues of concern, how negative interaction patterns increase, unacknowledged fears and negative emotions, and finally reframe key issues in terms of these negative patterns of interaction and underlying emotions and fears (Good Therapy, 2018; Ackerman, 2019b).

In the middle phases of treatment, known as the change events phase, the therapist and couple find ways to form new, stronger bonds in the relationship as well as create new emotional experiences to replace the negative experiences (Good Therapy, 2018; Ackerman, 2019b). In these sessions, individuals will be able to voice their attachment needs and deep emotions, partners learn ways to express acceptance, compassion, their attachment needs, and emotions as well as learn ways to discuss issues that may be a source of conflict (Good Therapy, 2018; Ackerman, 2019b).

The last phase, or consolidation of change phase, helps couples become better able to independently identify the attachment issues underlying conflict and to verbalize related emotions in future interactions (Good Therapy, 2018; Ackerman, 2019b). Therapists work with both partners in the use of new communication styles to discuss old issues and develop new solutions. Couples also learn ways to use their new skills outside of therapy and develop a plan to make new and consistent patterns of interaction (Good Therapy, 2018; Ackerman, 2019b).

**Hold Me Tight.** Hold Me Tight is a streamlined version of emotionally focused therapy that underlines the seven types of conversations couples can have that define their love relationship and outlines how these moments can be shaped to create a secure and lasting bond (Johnson, 2008). In the first two conversations, recognizing demon dialogue and finding the raw spots, couples identify negative and destructive comments to get to the root of the problem and figure out what each person is trying to say while looking beyond immediate, impulsive reactions (Johnson, 2019).

Next, revisiting a rocky moment, provides couples with a stage for de-escalating conflict, repairing rifts, and building emotional safety (Johnson, 2008). Hold Me Tight conversations move partners into being more accessible, emotionally responsive, and deeply engaged with each other, leading into forgiving injuries, which demonstrates renewal and connection, empowering couples to strengthen their bond (Johnson, 2008). Building off of this conversation is bonding through sex and touch, where couples learn how emotional connection creates great sex, and consequently, a deeper emotional connection is secured (Johnson, 2019).

The last conversation couples can have, keeping your love alive, is built on the understanding that love is a continual process of losing and finding emotional connection and helps couples be deliberate and mindful in maintaining the connection in their relationship (Johnson, 2008).

## EFT Techniques and Interventions

The techniques and interventions used in EFT mainly center around the principles of person-centered therapy and emotion coaching and a therapist trained in EFT will use several different techniques or interventions throughout therapy depending on what is appropriate in each situation (Ackerman, 2019b).

To engage with a couple and build a positive relationship, the therapist will begin with empathetic listening in which they make an attempt to connect with the couple to see things from each partner's perspective; thus, forming an authentic bond (Ackerman, 2019b). Normalizing, mirroring, or reflecting techniques will also be used during the session so that each individual feels understood and is able to grow and progress throughout therapy (Ackerman, 2019b).

Reframing individual experiences is essential to ensure the therapist understands the couple's problems correctly and can encourage each individual to see the issue from each other's perspective (Johnson, 2019). During EFT, therapists seek to piece together relevant details from conversations with the couple to recognize and understand any repetitive problem cycle that is occurring while, at the same time, redirecting the couple to the root of the problem when they become off-track (Ackerman, 2019b).

Each individual that is a part of EFT should feel that their emotions and experiences are understood; and therapists may find it necessary to encourage or stimulate certain emotions (Ackerman, 2019b). Each partner must also allow themselves to become vulnerable in order to effect change in the relationship (Johnson, 2019). Techniques that probe an individual's sensitive or particularly emotional experience can also be used to clarify vague or unclear aspects of an individual's or couple's experience (Ackerman, 2019b).

While providing encouragement and support, restructuring attempts may be made by a therapist to provoke new emotional experiences and lay a foundation for new, healthier interactions, using the knowledge and skills gained in therapy (Ackerman, 2019b). When couples find themselves in an old negative interactional cycle, they will be redirected by the therapist to apply the new strategies they have learned (Johnson, 2019). Towards the end of therapy, couples will make a plan for positive interaction in the future to ensure they do not move back towards old patterns once therapy has ended (Ackerman, 2019b).

**Solution-Focused Brief Therapy**

Solution-Focused Brief Therapy (SFBT) can be used in addition to other therapy styles to treat couples of all ages having a variety of issues to find quick solutions in the present while exploring a couple's hope for the future (Antin, 2019; Dolan, 2017; Lee, 2013). Working from the theory that all individuals are motivated to find solutions to improve their quality of life, SFBT first examines what an individual or couple is currently doing to initiate behavioral and lifestyle changes (Ackerman, 2018; Dolan, 2017).

Using interventions such as specific questioning techniques, 0-10 scales, empathy, and compliments, therapists help individuals to recognize their own virtues that have gotten them through difficult times in the past. Through these measures, individuals learn to focus on what they can do, rather than what they cannot, allowing them to quickly find solutions and make positive changes (Dolan, 2017)

Unlike other therapeutic methods, SFBT places an emphasis on finding quick solutions rather than analyzing problems in great detail. Problems are not addressed beyond a basic understanding and not every detail is examined, keeping the focus on finding a solution to the problem instead of discovering the root cause of the problem (Ackerman, 2018; Antin, 2019; Dolan, 2017).

Therapeutic sessions are routed in the present time and therapists work with both partners towards a future in which their current problem(s) has less of an impact (Ackerman, 2018; Antin, 2019). Conducting therapy in this manner allows the opportunity for quick relief from negative symptoms and minimizes the amount of time actually spent in therapy, as well as the time partners, suffer and struggle in their relationship (Ackerman, 2018; Antin, 2019).

Through SFBT, solutions to problems are discovered through the exceptions to the problem; more specifically, the times when the problem is not actively affecting the individual (Ackerman, 2018; Lee, 2013). Once an exception has been discovered, the therapist and couple will then work as a team to determine how the exception is different from the usual experiences with the problem, formulate a solution, set goals, and implement the solution (Ackerman, 2018).

SFBT therapists hold that focusing solely on a problem is not effective in finding a solution and firmly believes that targeting the default solution pattern, evaluating them for efficacy, and then modifying or replacing them with problem-solving approaches that work is more beneficial to a couple (Ackerman, 2018; Antin, 2019). Emphasis is placed on not only what the couple wants to change, but what is actually changeable and possible, knowing that the partners already have the resources and strengths to solve their problems (Ackerman, 2018; Antin, 2019; Dolan, 2017).

**SFBT techniques.** During an SFBT session, therapists will ask questions, notice and reinforce individual partner's positive qualities, strengths, resources, and general competence to solve their own problems, and work within what they can do rather than focusing on what they cannot (Ackerman, 2018; Antin, 2019). Helpful and effective behaviors that an individual is already engaging in will be drawn out and new ways to facilitate problem-solving will be explored through these behaviors to develop successful action plans (Ackerman, 2018; Antin, 2019).

At its very foundation, SFBT identifies and clarifies a couple's goals by questioning what they want out of therapy and specifically how their life would change after taking the necessary steps to resolve the identified problems (Antin, 2019; Dolan, 2017). Known as the "miracle question" the therapist will ask couples that if a miracle should occur, what changes would they notice in their life and relationship (Ackerman, 2018; Lee, 2013). By answering this question, couples can open their minds to creative thinking and begin to identify solutions, set goals, and create a plan leading to life-changing solutions (Ackerman, 2018; Dolan, 2017).

During therapy, SFBT therapists may also pose specific questions intended to provoke thinking and discussion about goal setting and problem-solving. Coping questions are designed to help partners recognize their own resiliency and identify ways in which they already effectively cope with their problems (Ackerman, 2018; Antin, 2019; Dolan, 2017). To identify the exceptions to the problem, therapists will also ask specific questions designed to probe an individual's experiences with and without the problem. This allows the provider to distinguish between the circumstances in which the problem is most active and when it holds no power or diminished power over the client's mood or thinking (Ackerman, 2018).

Scaling questions are sometimes used to ask individual partners to rate their experience (i.e. how the problem currently affects them) on a scale from 0 (lowest) to 10 (highest) to assist the therapist gauge progress and learn more about the individual's motivation and confidence in finding a solution (Ackerman, 2018; Antin, 2019; Dolan, 2017).

**Do one thing different.** Following a series of steps and thoughtfully answering a series of questions in the exercise, individuals learn how to break problem patterns, build strategies, recognize their strengths and resources, identify ways they can overcome the problem, and plan and set goals to address the problem (Ackerman, 2018).

**Presupposing change.** When couples are experiencing problems, they tend to focus on the problems and have difficulty recognizing the positive changes and occurrences in their life. The presupposing change technique is useful in assisting individuals be attentive to the positive things happening in their world, no matter how small or insignificant they may seem. This not only allows them to celebrate their successes but provides them a basis from which to facilitate future wins (Ackerman, 2018; Antin, 2019).

**Limitations of SFBT counseling.** There is the potential that partners will focus on problems that the therapist believes are secondary problems, such as focusing on a current relationship problem rather than the underlying self-esteem issue that is the underpinning of the problem in the relationship (Ackerman, 2018). During EFBT counseling, the therapist has to take what the partners say at face value, potentially leading to the of end treatment before they are convinced the couple is truly ready to end (Ackerman, 2018).

For the individuals undergoing SFBT therapy, its focus on quick solutions and the ability of individuals to fix their own problems, may miss important underlying issues and not allow for an emotional, empathetic connection between the therapist and client (Ackerman, 2018; Antin, 2019). Couples may become frustrated if they want to discuss factors outside of their immediate ability to affect change (Ackerman, 2018; Antin, 2019).

### Final Thoughts

It is important that partners in couples counseling understand that conflict is a natural and healthy part of their relationship, provided it is addressed in a positive manner. Attending therapeutic sessions will inevitably give each partner the necessary tools and techniques they need to improve their skills in conflict resolution, discuss sensitive topics, and to effectively communicate with each other, particularly during times of major life change and transition.

Building a secure and close connection between partners is essential to a successful relationship and a positive sense of self. Without this connection, relationships can be fueled by negativity that, unless treated, can lead to emotional distance, distress, loneliness, risk factors associated with mental health issues such as depression, anxiety, post-traumatic distress and substance addiction.

Therapeutic interventions such as attachment-based therapy, the Gottman Method, and emotionally focused therapy are used to gain a deeper insight into relationships by identifying and addressing individual's and couple's behaviors that help them maintain a positive orientation to each other and the relationship itself.

As an alternative to the more time-consuming in-depth therapy provided by these methods, couples can find quick solutions to their marital discord and unhappiness through solution-focused brief therapy, which focuses on what the couples want to change and provides them with the opportunity to use their own strength and resources to enact that change.

### Points to Remember

- *An individual's attachment style, developed in childhood, can determine how that individual acts and interacts in a relationship. Knowing a partner's attachment needs and having the ability to tune in to their emotions can help couples*

*reach a safe physical and emotional balance that promotes and nurtures an ideal relationship.*
- *Unhealthy behaviors, such as criticism, complaining, defensiveness, contempt, disgust, stonewalling, and/or mentally withdrawing, do not lend to a healthy relationship and often lead to additional mental and physical health concerns.*
- *Unlike other therapeutic interventions, solution-focused brief therapy is rooted in the present with a focus towards the future. Couples will gain quick relief from their problems and it minimizes the time spent in therapy although it may miss important underlying issues.*

# Chapter Seven

# Respecting Individual Differences: Strategies for Working with Special Populations

With the increase in diversity in today's population, the need for multicultural counseling has also increased. It is essential that all therapists possess the skills required to competently work with clients from a range of cultural backgrounds and approach counseling through the context of their client's world (Dore, 2016).

Counseling from a multicultural perspective allows therapists to help people in underserved communities, gain knowledge, sensitivity, disposition, and personal awareness by not only providing an understanding of the client's worldview, but insight to their own cultural values and biases (Online Counseling Programs, 2017). As such, the Association for Multicultural Counseling and Development (AMCD), among others, has publicized several competencies that therapists should aim to achieve in their counseling work with diverse clients (Arrendondo et al., 1996; Online Counseling Programs, 2017).

## Multicultural Competencies

It is imperative that therapists are aware of any cultural values or biases they possess and are able to acknowledge their own racial and cultural heritage and the effects of oppression, racism, discrimination, and stereotyping (Dore, 2016; Ratts, Singh, Butler, Nassar-McMillan, & McCullough, 2016; Ratts, Singh, Nassar-McMillan, Butler, & McCullough, 2015). As such, therapists should understand how these values and biases limit their practice and actively seek additional learning and professional development opportunities to improve their understanding of different cultural populations (Online Counseling Programs, 2017).

Therapists should recognize that their client's worldview is different than their own and be cognizant of their own emotional reactions to racial and ethnic groups different than their own. Therapists competent in multicultural counseling should also have an understanding of the population they work with and the ability to recognize that a client's race and culture influences their personality, decision-making skills, vocational choice, and reasons for or willingness to seek therapy (Online Counseling Programs, 2017; Ratts, 2016; Ratts, 2015).

**Culturally Appropriate Intervention Strategies**

A client's religious views, values, beliefs, culture, indigenous practices, and languages all have an impact on the therapeutic relationship (Online Counseling Programs, 2017). It is important that therapists know a client's family dynamics, hierarchy, bias in assessments, and discriminatory practices and be able to skillfully engage in verbal and nonverbal forms of communication that transcend a client's race or nationality, thereby eliminating any prejudice (Online Counseling Programs, 2017; Ratts et al., 2016; Ratts et al, 2015).

- **Perspective:** Therapists should possess the ability to view situations fluidly and from different perspectives so that they can truly understand the way clients interact with their environment and the way their environment interacts with them (Dore, 2016). These interactions can help therapists in understanding how the issues that brought the client to treatment are expressed, maintained, and potentially exacerbated (Dore, 2016).
- **Flexible Treatment:** Treatments should be modified or tailored to meet the needs of each client and therapists should keep in mind that certain words or vernacular may not resonate with all clients and potentially lead to rejection of the therapist and/or therapy itself (Dore, 2016.
- **Mindfulness:** Research theorizes that some components of mindfulness, such as self-awareness, compassion, nonjudgment, empathy, acceptance, and emotional intelligence, relate to or could foster aspects of multicultural counseling competence (Dore, 2016; Kabat-Zinn, 2005). Awareness, a principle found both in mindfulness practices and multicultural counseling competence, promotes a therapist's ability to understand cultural perspectives, including personal prejudices and biases (Kabat-Zinn, 2005).

- **Religious and Spiritual Awareness:** It is necessary for therapists to extract enough information to understand the purpose religion and spirituality have in their client's life as religion is inextricably linked to values and can define the context in which the individual lives (Dore, 2016).
- **The RESPECTFUL Model:** The RESPECTFUL model was developed to assist therapists in recognizing the multidimensionality of their clients in a comprehensive and integrative way. The model involves ten factors that can influence an individual's psychological development and sense of personal well-being. When taken into consideration by a therapist, this helps both the therapeutic sessions and the therapeutic relationship remain respectful, appropriate, and ethical (LeBeauf, Smaby, & Maddux, 2009).
- **Religious-Spiritual Identity:** For those clients that identify with a religion, they can be affected through transcendental experiences that extend beyond the ordinary (Online Counseling Programs, 2017).
- **Economic Background:** Both class standing and class roles can influence a client's development and therefore affect their own identification of strengths and expression of problems during therapeutic sessions (Online Counseling Programs, 2017).
- **Sexual Identity:** Research has shown that sexual identity influences personal development and likely reduce a client's sense of self-worth, particularly for those clients who have experienced oppression specifically due to their sexuality (Online Counseling Programs, 2017).
- **Psychological Maturity:** Psychological maturity is the ability of a client, based on psychological strengths and needs, to respond to a situation or environment in an appropriate manner (Online Counseling Programs, 2017).
- **Ethnic-Cultural-Racial Identity:** Client psychological development can be influenced by "within-group" differences (Ratts et al., 2015).
- **Chronological Developmental Challenges:** A client's physical, cognitive, and psychological skill development can affect how an individual experiences challenges at various points throughout their life (Online Counseling Programs, 2017).

- **Trauma and Threats to Well-Being:** Clients can be more at risk for psychological damage when faced with stressful situations and they have ineffective or diminished coping skills (Online Counseling Programs, 2017).
- **Family History and Dynamics:** Families are now more diverse, less rigid, and have broadened horizons and vision, all factors that play an integral role in how a client develops a sense of self, ambition, and prejudices (Ratts et al., 2015).
- **Unique Physical Characteristics:** Clients who possess unique physical characteristics may experience the stress of dissatisfaction and internalized negative views of stereotypes (Online Counseling Programs, 2017).
- **Residence Location and Language Differences:** A client's individual strengths can vary depending on the climate patterns, geological terrain, and types of occupations available (Online Counseling Programs, 2017). Inaccurate assumptions, stereotypes, and biases can occur when a client speaks a different language (Ratts et al., 2015).

**Multicultural Competence Counseling Model**

The first element of the multicultural competence counseling model requires therapists to be self-aware of the lens through which they view the world as the counseling profession requires therapists to assess normality and conceptualize clients' lives and behaviors through their own sense of normality, sense of right and wrong, and as a result of their own experiences and culture (Ginicola, 2014; Ratts et al., 2015). Therapists should examine how their attitudes, values, beliefs, and biases impact their worldview and their work with clients. Although some biases can be actively challenged and addressed, some are not adjustable, nor should they be (Ginicola, 2014; Ratts et al., 2016; Ratts et al., 2015).

Under the competence model, therapists should also be aware of their own social identities and statuses, and how power, privilege, oppression, and marginalization impact their worldview (Ginicola, 2014; Ratts et al., 2016; Ratts et al., 2015). Therapists should also endeavor to learn how privilege and marginalization impact worldview as well as how these statuses are linked to specific societal advantages and disadvantages (Ginicola, 2014; Ratts et al., 2016; Ratts et al., 2015).

Multicultural competency requires therapists to think reflectively and critically about their own assumptions and biases and be honest regarding where they hold privilege and marginalized identities. Therapists should have the ability to analyze and apply how these statuses impact their client and effectively communicate about privilege and marginalization in an effective, non-defensive manner (Ginicola, 2014; Ratts et al., 2016; Ratts et al., 2015).

The last section of the model requires therapists to actively build their self-awareness by pursuing formal professional development opportunities and attend trainings on marginalization and privilege to gain information about marginalized persons' experiences (Ginicola, 2014; Ratts et al., 2015). It is recommended that therapists pursue not only informal ways to connect to minority communities so that they can better understand their lives and experiences while building empathy (Ginicola, 2014; Ratts et al., 2015).

## Socioecological Model

It is important that therapists understand the sociocultural systems that their clients are a part of and how those systems are affecting their sense of well-being in order to effectively respond and address any issues during treatment (Ratts et al., 2016). The socioecological model of counseling provides a framework for therapeutic interventions and strategies at the intrapersonal, interpersonal, community, public policy, and international/global levels, allowing therapists to view client issues more contextually and determine whether goals for support need to occur individually or systemically (Ratts et al., 2016).

**Intrapersonal level.** At the intrapersonal level, multiculturally competent therapists are able to discuss their own cultures and identities, ask about their client's culture and identity, and facilitate open conversations related to how privileged and marginalized identities might act to enhance or barricade the therapeutic relationship (Ratts et al., 2016). Authentic, positive discussions surrounding this area can help therapists gain insight into their clients' cultural backgrounds and increase mutual trust, therefore deepening the therapeutic alliance (Ratts et al., 2016).

The exploration of a client's experiences with microaggressions and discrimination is also important at this level. Therapists are able to assist clients develop critical consciousness around experiences with racism, sexism, ableism, classism, religious oppression, and other "isms," which will facilitate a client's externalization of any oppression they have felt (Ratts et al., 2016).

It is crucial to a client's mental health and well-being that therapists are able to use culturally appropriate, empowerment-based frameworks and techniques to help their clients express powerful feelings of anger or despair that are a result of experiences with discrimination and oppression (Ratts et al., 2016).

**Interpersonal level.** At the interpersonal level, culturally competent therapists step outside the office setting and take the initiative to explore client relationships with family, friends, co-workers, and their community in order to identify any individuals that support or obstruct the client's progress (Ratts et al., 2016). It is essential that therapists assist clients in developing networks of caring individuals that share a similar privileged or marginalized identity and with whom they can identify (Ratts et al., 2016).

**Community level.** At this level, therapists should focus their attention on the norms and values in society and their influences on their clients' well-being by discussing how the clients believe others perceive them and if they believe that society holds negative stereotypes or attitudes about their membership in a privileged or marginalized group (Ratts et al., 2016).

**Public policy level.** Here, the focus is on rules, laws, and policies that impact clients and other members of their group. Therapists may undertake to alter oppressive laws and policies or help create more-inclusive policies (Ratts et al., 2016). Therapists may advocate with, or on behalf of, a client by using their own privilege to work with government officials to alter oppressive laws, policies, and practices and create those that foster diversity instead of perpetuate discrimination and stigmatization (Ratts et al., 2016).

**International/global level.** At the last level, therapists should endeavor to stay up to date on current events and seek knowledge on political and historical contexts through professional development opportunities in order to understand the impact that international activities may have on their clients, such as an increase in discrimination or hate crimes (Ratts et al., 2016).

## Client-Therapist Relationship

One of the most consistent and strong predictors of effective therapy and successful therapeutic outcomes is the quality of the client-therapist relationship (Fuertes, Brady-Amoon, Thind, & Chang, 2015). It is essential in working with multicultural clients to establish therapeutic trust and rapport by treating each client as an individual. This may require a modification in approach and timing to the working alliance in order to build trust and a bond between the therapist and client (Fuertes et al., 2015).

To begin building trust and rapport, it is essential to explore the client's perspective on the nature of therapy and the therapeutic relationship and use this understanding to assess and meet the needs and expectations that the client brings to therapy. Therapists should also ensure that the client feels understood by expressing openness to discussing the client's experiences, particularly those that were difficult or different and may have involved bias, oppression, and/or racism (Fuertes et al., 2015).

Validation is vital in this process and is essential to help clients begin to explore and process painful and difficult racial, cultural, or social experiences. Therapists should conduct regular check-ins with their clients to confirm their understanding of these experiences, always displaying empathy and respect for the client's cultural beliefs and perspectives, strengths, and resources (Fuertes et al., 2015).

Therapists must keep in mind that for some clients, racial, cultural, and other diversity factors may be central to therapy, but for others, these experiences may be peripheral or less relevant (Fuertes et al., 2015). Therapists should not generalize or stereotype a client into a profile based on their historical knowledge but approach the client as an individual who may have internalized particular values and beliefs that originated from a variety of environmental sources that include race, ethnicity, and culture. Treating a client as an individual personality who developed psychologically, socially, and culturally through a multitude of human relationships and experiences will foster a genuine and affirming therapeutic relationship (Fuertes et al., 2015).

It is necessary for therapists to understand that they may encounter difficulties in the therapeutic relationship and that there may be times where neither client nor therapist can be who they truly are. Clients may feel a lack of sensitivity or micro-aggression stemming from the therapist and believe that the therapist is not responding to or validating their experiences. In these situations, the difficulty could arise from the transference of past experiences, feelings, or relationships and thus, the client perceives or unconsciously experiences the therapist as a hurtful person from the past (Fuertes et al., 2015).

**Underserved Populations**

Underserved populations are groups of minorities, such as same-sex couples, ethnic minorities, and the physically impaired who face both daily struggles and lifelong challenges that impact them emotionally, physically, psychologically, and financially (Estes, 2017). It is incumbent upon therapists to educate themselves on the specific struggles of underserved populations and to consider the best approaches to helping their clients (Estes, 2017).

Therapists must keep in mind that underserved clients often arrive with layers of pain and emotional scars that are different from other clients in the sense that they have undergone negative impacts on their education, career, place of residence, and family as a result of their underserved status and have not typically had a safe space to talk about their experiences (Estes, 2017).

When working with underserved populations, therapists must create a safe space for their clients to discuss uncomfortable topics such as religion, ethnicity, or sexual preference and any accompanying rejection, physical and verbal attacks, and discrimination they have experienced (Estes, 20174). Open and honest discussions on sensitive topics will help clients own all parts of themselves and empower them to feel proud of who they are, to embrace their community, and to acknowledge the courage and strengths they have (Estes, 2017).

**Veterans**

Working with underserved populations in therapy can be challenging but therapists should keep in mind that working with veterans presents its own unique set of challenges (France, 2017). Due to their military background and hardship enduring mindset, veterans may find it difficult to reach out for help and to discuss their darkest and most intimate secrets with a stranger. It is essential that therapists aid veterans in understanding the necessity of processing the events they have experienced in and out of the military (Estes, 2017).

Veterans often fight an internal struggle between not wanting to admit needing help and recognizing that help is necessary and essential (Estes, 2017). When veterans finally do reach out for help, it is not to be proactive; rather, there is a significant challenge in their mind and/or environment that is more significant than any barriers to treatment (Estes, 2017). Therapists should be aware that at this point, while a veteran may be ready to discuss, process and understand their experiences; they may also want people to understand the experiences without having to talk about them (Estes, 2017).

Therapists should be extra vigilant in working with veterans to not express horror, condemnation, or revulsion at their experiences and to maintain a nonjudgmental point of view and unconditional positive regard (Estes, 2017). To build legitimacy, therapists should seek to develop an understanding of veterans and military culture and what is important to the veteran, knowledge beyond military acronyms and rank structure (Estes, 2017).

Of utmost importance, culturally competent therapists should not approach veterans as victims, heroes, or children (Estes, 2017). When veterans feel they are being treated as damaged and fragile or like they have to 'get over' their experiences, they will reject any help a therapist may provide and may put forth an increased resistance to it (Estes, 2017).

**Native Americans**

There are approximately 3 million Indigenous people in the United States, belonging to more than five hundred federally recognized nations, each with their own cultural practices and history (Roessel, 2018). The historical trauma of Indigenous people, whether it be massacres or forced relocations, has resulted in their struggle to maintain an identity; thus, causing subsequent intergenerational trauma (Roessel, 2018). As a result, Indigenous people experience higher rates of substance use and related disorders, PTSD, and suicide; for example, this minority is 526% more likely to die from alcohol use than are non-Indigenous people (Roessel, 2018).

Because Indigenous people feel stereotyped, ignored, and disrespected by non-Indigenous providers they are unlikely to seek out mental health care and many of the programs in existence that do serve Indigenous people are not culturally relevant or sensitive to the significant trauma within their communities (Roessel, 2018). Therapy, therefore, should be tailored to the individual and clients should be met where they are at (Roessel, 2018).

When working with Indigenous people and taking into account past incidences of trauma, therapists should place PTSD high on their list for differential diagnosis, being careful not to misdiagnose it as depression or borderline personality (Roessel, 2018). Intergenerational trauma, including the loss of sacred lands, forced assimilation, and family ruptures, should be acknowledged and the strength of survivors should be emphasized and validated (Roessel, 2018).

**Disabled**

Negative attitudes, historical beliefs, lack of knowledge about disabilities, and associations pertaining to individuals with disabilities as diseased, broken, and in need of repair, can extend beyond the general public and into the therapist's office, thus impacting the relationship between therapist and client (Stuntzner & Hartley, 2014).

When working with clients with disabilities, therapists should first examine their own beliefs and expectations about disability, disability types, and anticipated outcomes (American Psychological Association, 2019; Stuntzner & Hartley, 2014). Most importantly, therapists should, through self-examination, determine whether they view a client with disabilities as an individual who has the same rights, needs, and desires as a client without a disability or if they perceive the client as incapable, weak, less than, suffering, pitiful, handicapped, or physically/mentally challenged (American Psychological Association, 2019; Stuntzner & Hartley, 2014).

Most therapists do not have a first-hand understanding of a client's disability experience and may feel anxious, repulsed, fearful, and vulnerable when working with a client who has a disability and thus makes erroneous assumptions about their client. They may assume that a client with a disability must have certain related characteristics (American Psychological Association, 2019). Therapists may also over-emphasize or mistakenly focus on a client's disability while ignoring important aspects of their life, such as capabilities, strengths, and other life events (American Psychological Association, 2019). Conversely, therapists may under-emphasize disability-related concerns or even assume clients use their disabilities as an excuse (American Psychological Association, 2019).

Therapists have a responsibility to be cognizant of their own word-choice and use of terms when referring to clients with disabilities. Outdated or inaccurate words can encourage and promote poor and negative perceptions and feelings about clients with disabilities and can influence the way clients view themselves (Stuntzner & Hartley, 2014). Therapists should also be cognizant of the fact that clients with disabilities may have other preferences and ways for identifying and describing themselves and should not assume that the client's chosen way of self-identification is how the therapist can refer to the individual (Stuntzner & Hartley, 2014).

To develop an effective therapeutic relationship, therapists should treat clients with disabilities as human beings rather than as their disability, keeping in mind that labels can affect a client's emotional well-being (American Psychological Association, 2019; Stuntzner & Hartley, 2014). Therapists should pay particular attention to the strengths and abilities of the client and incorporate them into the counseling relationship. Therapists can help clients with disabilities by teaching them to redefine their self-concept and self-identity, how to self-advocate, and how to integrate these learned skills to become more empowered (American Psychological Association, 2019). Research has shown that assisting clients with forgiveness, self-compassion, and resiliency can reduce negative emotions and improve overall functioning and well-being (Stuntzner & Hartley, 2014).

It is also important for therapists to consider how a client's disability interacts with cultural and social identities and experiences as different cultural, religious and underserved groups may attribute different causes and meanings to disability (American Psychological Association, 2019). Some groups, for example, believe that having a disability is a gift or challenge while others see it as punishment or fate.

## LGBTQ+

Prior to working with LGBTQ+ clients, therapists should recognize how their attitudes, implicit and explicit biases, and knowledge about LGBTQ+ issues may be relevant to assessment and treatment and attempt to evaluate their competencies and limitations of expertise. Without a high level of awareness about their own beliefs, values, needs, and limitations, therapists may actually impede the progress of a client in therapy (American Psychological Association, 2019; Lytle, Vaughan, Rodriguez, Shmerler, 2014).

Therapists can help promote mental health well-being for LGBTQ+ clients by actively removing the stigma that homosexuality is a mental illness but before doing so, must understand that societal stigmatization, prejudice and discrimination can be sources of stress and create concerns about personal security for LGBTQ+ clients (American Psychological Association, 2019). As such, to effectively work with LGBTQ+ clients, therapists should not only create a sense of safety in the therapeutic environment but should also assess the client's history of victimization as a result of harassment, discrimination, and violence, particularly for those clients that are part of more than one cultural minority (Lytle, Vaughan, Rodriguez, Shmerler, 2014).

It is critical for therapists working with clients that have multiple minority statuses to display sensitivity to the complex dynamics associated with other overlapping layers of social identities and statuses (e.g., social class, gender roles, religious beliefs) (American Psychological Association, 2019; Lytle, Vaughan, Rodriguez, Shmerler, 2014). Therapists should strive to assist their clients in recognizing effective coping strategies and other protective factors that their LGBTQ+ clients from racial, ethnic, cultural and other minority backgrounds may have developed from their multiple marginalization experiences (Lytle et al., 2014).

Interventions that may be useful include increasing the client's sense of safety, reducing stress, developing resources, resolving residual trauma, and empowering the client to confront social stigma and discrimination, when appropriate and safe to do so (American Psychological Association, 2019; Lytle et al., 2014; Society of Clinical Psychology, 2016).

## Final Thoughts

It is critical that all therapists have the requisite multicultural competency skills to competently work with an increasingly diverse population. Counseling and therapy should always be approached through the context of the client's world and in order to do so, therapists must be aware of any cultural values or biases they hold as well as the effect oppression, racism, discrimination, and stereotyping may have on their clients.

Therapy should always be approached through the client's worldview and multiculturally competent therapists have the ability to view each client and their individual situation fluidly and from different perspectives. Understanding the way a client interacts with their environment as well as how they express, maintain, minimize, and/or exacerbate an issue, can assist therapists in framing and comprehending the issues that led the individual to seek out therapy in the first place. It is essential that the therapist also considers the complex dynamics associated with clients that hold multiple minority statuses and overlapping layers of social identities.

When working with multidimensional and underserved clients, models such as the RESPECTFUL Model, Multicultural Competence Counseling Model, and Socioecological Model of Counseling serve as invaluable guidance to maintaining a multiculturally competent practice that remains respectful, appropriate, and ethical. Under these models, therapists must treat all clients as individual human beings that have specific struggles due to their unique situations and specific attention should be given to a client's strengths, abilities, and emotional well-being.

## Points to Remember

- *Multiculturally competent therapists understand the population they work with and have the ability to recognize that a client's race and culture will influence personality, decision-making skills, and reasons for or willingness to seek therapy*

- *Competent therapists understand their own assumptions, biases, social identities, and statuses and that power, privilege, oppression, and marginalization impact not only their worldview, but how they view their clients.*
- *Culturally appropriate, empowerment-based frameworks and techniques help their clients express any powerful feelings that are an outcome of experiences with discrimination and oppression.*
- *Effective therapists establish therapeutic trust and rapport by treating each client as an individual and acknowledge that for some clients, race, culture, and other diversity factors may be central to therapy, but not for others. As such, therapists should not generalize or stereotype a client based on their own historical knowledge.*
- *Successful therapy creates safe spaces for the open and honest discussion of uncomfortable topics and helps clients to become empowered and proud of who they are and to acknowledge their courage and strengths.*

# Chapter Eight

# Understanding the Value of the Therapist: Change Agent Characteristics that Promote Positive Outcomes

Outcome studies in psychotherapy have consistently shown that the therapist is the key to change and that there are numerous factors among effective therapists that are consistently related to successful therapy outcomes (Firestone, 2019; Miller, 2017). Evidence also shows that the primary determinants of positive results in therapy stem from human and relational elements (Elkins, 2015).

Therapists who are high in empathy, low in defensiveness, able to endure strong client emotions, and can encourage the development of new coping skills, maintain healthy interpersonal boundaries, and mildly confront clients with problematic behaviors and attitudes are more effective than their peers who lack these skills and qualities (Miller, 2015; 2017). Research shows that these therapists are effective, and their clients experience 50% more improvement, 50% less drop out, have shorter lengths of stay, and are significantly less likely to deteriorate while in therapy (Miller, 2015).

Successful therapy begins with the provider's focus on the personal and cultural needs of the client to determine the best therapeutic approach, taking care not to impose their particular brand on clients. Instead, effective therapists enter into a collaborative discussion with the client to determine what type of therapeutic approach best fits their needs (Elkins, 2015).

### Theoretical Orientation

Each model of therapy, such as psychoanalytic, cognitive-behavioral, client-centered, and mindfulness-based, has its own assumptions about why people become distressed and what techniques are likely to be helpful (Miller, 2017). Research has uncovered the 'Dodo Bird Verdict' which states that all major forms of psychotherapy are equally effective in reducing distress and improving mental health (Johnson, 2018; Miller, 2017; Wampold, 2011). Evidence has been found that various treatments for depression, alcohol use disorders, PTSD, and childhood disorders are equally effective (Hall, 2015; Wampold, 2011). It is not the specific model of therapy that a therapist uses that will predict successful client outcomes; rather, it is the therapist characteristics, therapeutic alliance, and the therapeutic relationship (Johnson, 2018; Miller, 2017; Simon, 2016; Meyers, 2014; Wampold, 2011).

Effective therapists do not attempt to fit their clients into the mold of a particular theoretical model but try to learn from them and develop a uniquely personal psychological theory for each individual client by subordinating their own interests and directing their attention and efforts toward understanding their clients (Firestone, 2019; Kvarnstrom, 2015).

- **Credentials:** Research suggests that whether a client sees a social worker (MSW, LCSW), a counselor (MA), a Marriage and Family Therapist (MFT), a psychologist (Ph.D., Psy.D., or Ed.D.), or a psychiatrist (MD) for therapy, the particular degree the therapist possesses has little relationship to their competence (Johnson, 2018; Miller, 2017).
- **Deliberate Practice:** The most effective therapists do not take shortcuts and are not on the fast track to success; rather, they seek to improve client outcomes and positive results by spending an average of 2.5 to 4.5 more hours per week outside of work in activities specifically designed to improve the effectiveness of their work (Miller, 2015).
- **Self-Awareness:** Self-awareness has a major impact on a therapist's effectiveness and as such, therapists should look within themselves to identify their own unmet psychological needs and desires so they can prevent those issues from affecting or conflicting with those of their clients (Hall, 2015; Miller, 2018). Therapists would use the self-awareness of their own emotions to identify with a client and respond sensitively to their struggles (Firestone, 2019). Successful therapists are aware of how their own background, personality, and status can interact with the background, personality, and status of the client, particularly in terms of the client reaction to the therapist, the therapist reaction to the client, and to their overall interaction (Wampold, n.d.).

- **Authenticity:** The ideal therapist is an authentic role model that holds high regard for honesty and integrity, has developed a considerable amount of self-knowledge and recognizes and accepts an objective view of both the negative and positive traits contained within their own personality (Firestone, 2019).
- **Multicultural Competency:** It is important that effective therapists display multicultural competence, embrace a multicultural worldview, and have the ability to understand their clients regardless of the client's race, ethnicity, religious or political beliefs, and/or socioeconomic background (Arrendondo, 1996; Dutch, 2019; Miller, 2015; 2018; Meyers, 2014). Equally important, an effective therapist should be culturally aware and recognize that every relational encounter and interaction with a client is a multicultural encounter in which they can learn from their clients (Elkins, 2015)
- **Acceptance:** Therapists must begin where the client is, relate to the client in a warm, understanding, open, and nonjudgmental manner, and accept the individual for who they are in the current situation; doing so will instill a sense of trust between the therapist and client and create a safe environment in which the client can share their innermost thoughts and fears (Elkins, 2015; Firestone, 2019; Kvarnstrom, 2015; Meyers, 2014).
- **Warmth:** It is important for the client to feel both invited into and comfortable with the therapy process, particularly those clients that are reluctant or cautious when it comes to therapy (Simon 2016). When a therapist displays warmth and shows empathy that weaves seamlessly with care and concern, the difficult endeavor into the therapeutic process may become more endurable for the client and sustain a successful outcome (Simon, 2016; Elkins, 2015).
- **Empathy:** Compassion and empathy, whether it be conveyed orally, through eye contact, posture, or tone of voice are both essential to the healing process, in building the therapist-client bond and in helping clients feel understood and heard (Dutch, 2019; Miller, 2017; 2018; Rauch, 2016). For therapy to be successful, discussions and the potential confrontation that can arise when delving into difficult and sensitive topics must be benign, free from any malice or ill intent on behalf of the therapist and rooted

solely in a sincere desire to help the client (Simon, 2016; Elkins, 2015).

- **Communication Skills:** Effective therapists should have a wide array of excellent communication skills as well as the natural ability to listen to clients, understand what they are saying, and clearly explain their ideas and thoughts (Elkins, 2015; Miller, 2018; Rauch, 2016). The therapist should be able to communicate with clients in a meaningful way that leaves them feeling welcomed, supported, and accepted (Kvarnstrom, 2015; Meyers, 2014).
- **Rapport-Building Skills:** It is critical that therapists possess a strong set of interpersonal skills to establish rapport and develop strong relationships with their clients (Miller, 2018). To cultivate a sense of trust with their client, therapists must actively listen, place all of their focus on what the client is discussing, avoid being distracted, and provide their undivided attention (Dutch 2019; Miller, 2018).
- **Flexibility:** Effective therapists provide their clients with a flexible treatment plan that fosters a sense of hopefulness and motivation as well as encourages the client to act in a healthy manner, monitoring progress and adapting and changing how they respond in order to meet the client's needs (Miller, 2018; Wampold, n.d.). Although a successful therapist can be persuasive, clients may be resistant to treatment or not make adequate progress and as such, it is necessary that the therapist be aware of verbal and nonverbal cues, use the evidence from assessing therapeutic progress, take in new information, test hypotheses, and be willing to be wrong (Wampold, n.d.). In situations of resistance, therapists must be flexible and make adjustments, although sometimes subtle, in the way treatments are presented, in the theoretical approach used, and/or in the use of adjunctive services, such as medication (Wampold, n.d.).
- **Problem-Solving Skills:** To effectively assist clients, therapists must be able to identify and make changes to a client's negative thought patterns and other harmful behaviors without injecting their own material into therapy unless doing so is done with deliberateness and positively contributes to the therapeutic process (Miller, 2018; Wampold, n.d.). Therapists should endeavor to reflect on their own reactions to the client to determine if their

reactions are reasonable given the client's presentation or are based on the therapist's own issues (Wampold, n.d.).
- **Client-centered:** Clients should be regarded as a partner in the client-therapist relationship. An effective therapist will seek to gather routine feedback on how the client feels about therapy and the therapist (Elkins, 2015; Kvarnstrom, 2015; Meyers, 2014). Therapists can display caring towards a client by sharing emotional feedback via facial expressions or statements and practical feedback, including suggestions on new ways of thinking, assessing relationships, and improving mental health outside of therapy (Rauch, 2016).
- **Directiveness:** Effective therapists are leaders who have the insight on which direction the client needs to move in, behavioral changes that need to be made, and coping mechanisms that need to be learned and can be clearly directive in their approach and outline the small, yet necessary, steps the client needs to accomplish in order to move forward in the therapeutic process (Ponton, 2018; Simon, 2016). Once clients are on the right path, the therapist must take steps to help them stay on that path by redirecting the client and returning them to the path when they invariably stray away from it (Simon, 2016).
- **Reward:** A client's positive efforts and any steps in the right direction should be rewarded and reinforced no matter how small or insignificant they are. Not only does an effective therapist encourage new and adaptive behavior, they recognize the value and attach the appropriate merits to it so the client can gain the necessary motivation to replace troublesome habits with new and improved habits (Simon, 2016).
- **Optimism:** Therapists should be aware of clients' propensity to turn against themselves and act on their critical inner voices, paying particular attention to the relationship between past experiences and present disturbances (Firestone, 2019). To support clients and empower their own self-healing, focus should be given to client strengths and resources as well as creating client attributes, such as communication skills and a positive attitude that will facilitate their ability to solve their own problems (Elkins, 2015; Meyers 2014; Ponton, 2018). Effective therapists remain optimistic, hold a strong belief that clients can personally grow and change, instill hope in their clients, do

not underestimate the strength of a client's defense systems, and are sensitive to their clients' fears regarding change, particularly at crucial points in the therapeutic process (Firestone, 2019; Rauch, 2016; Wampold, n.d.).

## Therapeutic Relationship and Therapeutic Alliance

Research confirms that the therapeutic relationship is essential to a therapy client's success and is one of the most important factors in successful therapy outcomes independent of the specific type of treatment (Dutch, 2019; Firestone, 2016; Johnson, 2018). Therapeutic alliance, an integral part of the therapeutic relationship, involves the therapeutic bond that is created when the therapist and client collaboratively and purposely work together to create an essential agreement about the goals of therapy and treatment tasks and the client feels understood, validated, and supported (Hall, 2015; Meyers, 2014). The strength of this alliance between the client and therapist has been found to be a better predictor of therapeutic success and positive client outcomes than the specific kind of therapy and the qualities and characteristics of the therapist (Gurton, 2019; Kvarnstrom, 2015).

As authentic humans, effective therapists will display a deep interest in their clients as individuals and will see and relate to them in a sensitive and tailored manner specific to individual needs (Firestone, 2016). To establish a solid relationship built on trust and understanding, the therapist must be attuned to the client's state of being (Firestone, 2016). In this way, working alliances can be formed where a broad range of clients feel understood, trust the therapist, and believe that the therapist can actually help (Hall, 2015; Rauch, 2016).

Successfully attuned therapists will be able to offer their clients a new perspective of themselves and of relationships in general (Firestone, 2016). According to attachment theory, the greatest predictor of a client's attachment patterns in their relationships is the one they experienced growing up and that relationship is the one that shapes the reactions they have as an adult (Firestone, 2016). To form healthier relationships and more secure attachments as part of the therapeutic process, clients need to develop an understanding of themselves through a coherent narrative that can only be told as part of a successful alliance with the therapist (Firestone, 2016).

Research demonstrates that when a client forms a secure attachment to the therapist, the individual reveals their real self, recognizes wants and needs, what changes need to occur, and therefore, experiences a significant reduction in stress, feels safe in beginning to resolve traumas, and evolves in their model of relating (Firestone, 2016). More specifically, a positive therapeutic alliance has been found to reduce suicide attempts in clients with borderline personality disorder, reduce symptoms in chronically depressed patients, and promote a greater adherence to treatment in clients with bipolar disorder (Kvarnstrom, 2015).

To enact change and assist clients in fulfilling their wants and needs, the therapist should provide clients with an acceptable and adaptive explanation that is compatible with the clients' attitudes, values, culture, and worldview, take into account the context of the clients (i.e. culture, race, ethnicity), and provide a means for the clients to overcome their difficulties (Dutch, 2019; Firestone, 2016; Meyers, 2014; Rauch, 2016; Wampold, n.d.).

In addition to counselor characteristics and the therapeutic relationship, positive therapy outcomes are achieved through quality client participation (Johnson, 2018). A client's active participation in therapy through involvement learning, and the application of what is learned in therapy, leads to a successful and positive therapy experience. Clients must be motivated, open to exploring their emotions and internal experiences as well as willing to endure any discomfort and make efforts to achieve change to improve outcomes (Johnson, 2018).

## Final Thoughts

Positive therapeutic outcomes begin with a focus on the personal and cultural needs of the client and a collaborative discussion to determine the best therapeutic approach to address the client's presenting problem(s). No matter which style of therapy is selected for use, all are equally effective in reducing distress and improving mental health. Neither one is better than the other in terms of predicting successful outcomes.

There are a variety of human and relational elemental factors that are consistently predictive of successful outcomes and positive results in therapy. Research shows that therapists who possess these attributes have clients that experience more improvement, attend therapy more and for shorter amounts of time, and are significantly less likely to deteriorate while in therapy. Key characteristics of an effective therapist include self-awareness, authenticity, empathy, multicultural competence and, most importantly, the ability to build and nurture a therapeutic relationship and alliance.

Compassion and empathy, along with effective communication, are also essential in developing positive outcomes. Given the therapist's ability to effectively communicate, understand the client, and explain their ideas and thoughts in a meaningful way, clients will not only feel welcomed into the therapeutic relationship, but feel they are accepted, heard, understood, and supported. As a result of these therapist characteristics and the collaborative work done between the therapist and client, a therapeutic bond and alliance is built and as a result, becomes the best predictor of therapeutic success and positive client outcomes.

## Points to Remember

- *It is not the specific model of therapy that a therapist uses that will predict successful client outcomes, but therapist characteristics, therapeutic alliance, and the therapeutic relationship.*
- *Successful therapists are self-aware and not only know how their own emotions, backgrounds, personality, and status effect, and/or conflict with, their relationship with the client but know how to use their emotions, background, personality, and status to identify, understand, and empathize with their client.*
- *Multicultural competence and the therapist's ability to understand clients regardless of their race, ethnicity, religious beliefs, ability, and/or socioeconomic background is essential and allows the therapist to meet the clients where they are, accept them for who they are, and relate to them in an understanding, open, and nonjudgmental manner, creating a trusting and safe environment for therapy.*
- *Effective therapists provide flexible treatment approaches that foster hope and provide motivation and encouragement, monitor client progress, seek feedback, and adapt their responses to meet the client's needs.*
- *Therapists who achieve the most positive outcomes acknowledge their clients' strengths and help them develop positive attributes that will empower self-healing, believe in positive change and growth, and are sensitive to a client's fear of change.*

# Chapter Nine

# Contemporary Therapeutic Approaches: Cutting-Edge Practices with Promise

In today's society, one in five Americans is diagnosed with some form of mental illness and 56% of them do not receive proper treatment (Gleit, 2017; Richards, 2018). There are a number of obstacles that prevent individuals from receiving care, including provider shortages, finances, unwillingness to seek treatment due to stigma, and lack of access to care (Gleit, 2017; Richards, 2018). It is noteworthy that in 2016, 34.3 million adults self-reported needing treatment for alcohol or drug use and/or mental health treatment; yet, there were over 100 million individuals without adequate access to mental health services due to over 4600 designated mental health shortage areas across the country (Gleit, 2017).

Advances in technology have removed many of these obstacles. Counseling websites offer individuals in need of treatment access to licensed, experienced therapists, therapy by phone, chat, message board, video, and mobile apps, and are HIPAA compliant (E-Counseling, 2019). Clients also have the ability to connect with a therapist outside their area and change therapists if the relationship is not the right fit (E-Counseling, 2019).

Online counseling can provide help 24/7, remove any associated stigmatization, and affords clients complete privacy and confidentiality (E-Counseling, 2019). Therapists are bound by strict local and federal laws, including HIPAA, and conversations are secured by various levels of encryption. To be more comfortable, clients can also sign up using a false name and e-mail account (E-Counseling, 2019).

### Online Cognitive Behavioral Therapy

Nearly half of primary care physicians treat mental health conditions and through telehealth can now offer online cognitive behavioral therapy (iCBT) (Richards, 2018). iCBT uses cognitive and behavioral techniques utilized in traditional face-to-face therapy for treating mental health issues and is composed of education, skills training, activities and exercises that promote the application of new knowledge and coping skills (Richards, 2018). Structured modules of content are delivered using text, pictures, animations, audio files and videos that can be completed by the client at any time, from anywhere (Richards, 2018).

One of the advantages of iCBT is that it combats the shortage of accessible mental healthcare providers, particularly in rural areas where some states, such as Alabama, have a 1 to 260 clinician-to-patient ratio (Richards, 2018). It also alleviates lengthy wait times; for example, some clients have waited an average of 66 days to see a physician for a traditional face-to-face visit (Richards, 2018).

Physicians are able to enroll patients immediately and identify a need, promote continuity of care, and increase clinical workflow (Richards, 2018). Research has demonstrated that individuals using web-based therapy and online treatments as a supplement are more likely to remain engaged in face-to-face therapy (Richards, 2018).

For the treatment of mild to moderate mental health conditions, iCBT has demonstrated the ability to offer services to six times as many patients while generating the same outcomes, allowing healthcare providers to offer programs across their entire population, minimizing valuable resources and enabling hospitals to better triage patients (Richards, 201).

iCBT is also a less expensive option than more traditional therapy. Typically, patients move through online content at a self-administered pace, reducing the amount of clinical support time required and eliminating the need for patients to take time off from work (Richards, 2018). In the future, iCBT may also ease the strain put on emergency services for the treatment of behavioral health (Richards, 2018).

## Mental Health Applications

There are now more than 10,000 mental health-related smartphone applications (apps) and their rapid rise is due in part to their potential to transform a client's phone into a monitoring and therapeutic program capable of capturing real-time mental health symptoms and delivering immediate therapy (Torous, Luo, & Chan, 2018). Apps focused on protecting or improving mental health use methods such as meditation, hypnosis, and cognitive behavioral therapy (CBT), as well as provide a valuable support network for those seeking online therapy (Nichols, 2018).

One such app, Calm, is designed to reduce anxiety by focusing on the four key areas of meditation, breathing, sleep, and relaxation; while another app called Headspace uses mindfulness and meditation to reduce stress, improve focus and attention, and enhance compassionate behavior towards others (Nichols, 2018). Other apps provide online therapy using trained listeners and licensed therapists who are available 24/7 for anonymous, nonjudgmental emotional support. Those in need can search for therapists based on experience or specialties, such as anxiety, depression, stress, PTSD, eating disorders, and relationship issues (Nichols, 2018).

Despite the prevalence of mental health apps, there is no evidence they are evidence-based or effective (Torous et al., 2018). Evidence-based reviews of suicide prevention and bipolar apps have identified a few potentially harmful sites, some offering dangerous and harmful advice (Torous et al., 2018). Other studies on mental health applications, however, have demonstrated efficacy and improved treatment outcomes for disorders such as schizophrenia, depression, anxiety disorders, and suicidal ideation (Torous et al., 2018). Research conducted with individuals suffering from schizophrenia noted that some individuals used their smartphones to play music to block auditory hallucinations (Torous et al., 2018).

Unlike methods of therapy that use specific protocols, mental health applications are a personal choice, dynamic, and constantly changing, resulting in different versions, differing reviews, and invalid rating systems (Torous et al., 2018). As such, the American Psychological Association (2018) has developed an evaluation model that therapists and clients alike can use in determining if a mental health app is appropriate and beneficial for use.

**American Psychological Association Evaluation Model**

Any mental health applications credibility must first be determined by establishing who made it, how much it costs, and its technology requirements (American Psychological Association, 2018; Torous et al., 2018). Next, the risk, privacy, and security features of the app must be assessed as many mental health apps actively aim to avoid falling under U.S. federal health care privacy rules, such as the Health Insurance Portability and Accountability Act of 1996 (HIPAA), therefore leaving clients' personal mental health information unprotected and often sold for profit (American Psychological Association, 2018; Torous et al., 2018). Users of mental health apps should make sure that any sensitive data is protected through digital encryption and secure storage (Torous et al., 2018).

Third, consumers of mental health apps should seek to find one with a clinically verifiable evidence of effectiveness; and similarly, therapists should try an app before recommending it to a client to ensure it indeed does what it claims to do, while not offering any dangerous or harmful recommendations (American Psychological Association, 2018). It is essential that therapists also consider how engaging and usable the app will be for their client, particularly since research shows that engagement with mental health apps rapidly declines over the first week of use (American Psychological Association, 2018).

Lastly, it is important to determine if the data collected and/or generated by the app is available to the therapist, client, and any other individual involved in the client's care. Apps that fragment care by not sharing information have actually been shown to impede care and hamper society's move towards integrated care (Torous et al., 2018).

**Blogs.** Mental health blogs are not only used to educate people about mental health conditions and challenges, they can help stop the stigma surrounding mental illnesses (American Counseling Association, 2014). Over the last 30 years, research has shown that short-term focused writing about emotions has not only many physical benefits, such as enhanced immune function, lower blood pressure, and decreased heart rate, but also mental health benefits including lowered anxiety, less rumination, increased self-esteem, less social anxiety, less emotional distress, and fewer depressive symptoms (American Counseling Association, 2014).

Blogging can be anonymous by nature and may assist individuals in expressing themselves more freely; yet, it is recommended that these thoughts and feelings also be discussed in therapy. Bloggers must also keep in mind that the comment sections of blogs can be extremely negative and hurtful and comment moderation tools should be used by both therapists and clients alike (American Counseling Association, 2014).

It is of utmost importance that therapists are aware of blogs and websites that promote harmful behaviors and that if a client discloses talking to others online, they should investigate the nature of the communications to determine if they are supportive or destructive in nature (Boodman, 2015).

**Video games.** Despite the controversy over video games, research shows they may have the potential to provide a gateway to more effective therapeutic relationships and foster more positive clinical outcomes when used in combination with other forms of therapy (Reardon, 2015). One of the major benefits of video game play is that players are able to expand their social support networks and engage with diverse groups of people (Reardon, 2015; Vitelli, 2014).

Games may assist players in developing motivation and persistence and giving them a safe place to practice the regulation of negative emotions such as anger, anxiety, frustration, and sadness (Reardon, 2015). A European research study, for example, found that a video game designed to help clients with impulse control improved emotional regulation and impulsivity (Reardon, 2015).

Not only can video games help improve mood and lead to positive feelings, they can distract players from real-world problems, reduce anxiety, and increase relaxation (Vitelli, 2014). Flow experiences, where gamers feel fully mentally immersed in the game without feeling self-conscious, have been linked to positive outcomes such as greater self-esteem and a sense of achievement that can translate to greater mental health benefits (Vitelli, 2014). Experiencing positive emotions during gameplay can also increase desirable behaviors, build social relationships that provide support for achieving goals and coping with failure, and counteract the effects of negative emotions (Vitelli, 2014).

Although many video games can be violent in nature, they may provide players with an opportunity to learn social skills by cooperating with team members. Research has shown that playing games in groups reduces feelings of hostility and has the potential to curb antisocial thoughts and behaviors (Vitelli 2014).

Video games have the potential to educate others on the experience of mental illness (Cheang & Doshi, 2017). The game Hellblade: Senua's Sacrifice, depicts a woman who lives with psychosis (Lacina, 2017). Using auditory, visual, and tactile effects, the game reinforces the reality that Senua's illness cannot be fixed and that recovery is not always a straight path (Lacina, 2017). Vulnerability is not synonymous with a lack of strength and the game shows players that strength can come from an individual's determination to push through times of crisis and survive (Cheang & Doshi, 2017). There is some debate, however, if the game actually "invalidates real experiences" (Lacina, 2017, n.p.).

Research confirms that the majority of individuals who suffer from mental illness are not violent and are actually 10 times more likely to be victims of violent crime (Cheang & Doshi, 2017). One of the most important features of Hellblade is the fact that Senua is never presented as a violent individual nor is her experience ever questioned or invalidated (Cheang & Doshi, 2017). Whether or not the events, games, and characters in the game occurred in objective reality is irrelevant as they are real to Senua and cause her significant harm. Players learn through the game that what matters most is how they choose to live with that reality and accept it in order to progress (Cheang & Doshi, 2017).

## Advantages of Therapy and Counseling Online

**Accessibility**

With online therapy, clients living in remote areas with fewer mental health services, clients with rigid schedules, or those with physical conditions making travel difficult now have greater access to the services they need (Alliant International University, 2019; Azam, 2017; Cherry, 2018; Gleit, 2017; Tomikawa, 2017). Individuals suffering from depression, anxiety, and other disorders now have a more convenient option to make their therapy sessions with no travel required and reduced stress (Beasley, 2019).

Clients suffering from depression who are fatigued and overwhelmed as well as those with physical disabilities, have easy access to the therapist without having to leave the house (Beasley, 2019; Cherry, 2018; Gleit, 2017). For clients with social anxiety, there is no longer the need to sit in front of a stranger to share their thoughts and feelings, they can do it from the privacy of their own home in a multitude of ways, such as writing the therapist instead of a live session (Azam, 2017; Beasley, 2019).

**Flexibility**

Online counseling provides clients with the flexibility to talk at scheduled times that are convenient as well as during unexpected stressful situations (Alliant International University, 2019; Beasley, 2019; Cherry, 2018; Tomikawa, 2017). Clients have the option to write to their therapist when an upsetting issue occurs and obtain feedback later in the day rather than having to wait until their next scheduled session, often more than a week away (Beasley, 2019).

**Effectiveness**

Research has shown that virtual mental health counseling is at least as effective, if not more so, at treating depression as traditional face-to-face counseling (Gleit, 2017; Richards, 2018). According to a study done by the University of Zurich, depression was eased in 53% of the individuals given online therapy versus 50% of the clients who had online counseling and three months post-study, 57% of online therapy clients showed no signs of depression compared to 42% of conventional therapy clients (Gleit, 2017). A four-year study of 100,000 veterans conducted by Johns Hopkins found that the number of days patients were hospitalized dropped 25% if they chose online counseling, slightly higher than the number of hospital visits experienced by patients who chose traditional counseling (Gleit, 2017).

## Disadvantages of Therapy and Counseling Online

### Dependency

Although online therapy can beneficially broaden the means of communication between therapist and client through text messaging, emails, and the sharing of multimedia content, these activities can raise issues of unclear boundaries and limits of confidentiality (Azam, 2017; Keenan, 2016). The range of communication with clients can become ambiguous and difficult to manage and can prompt inappropriate expectations in the realm of social media (Azam, 2017; Keenan, 2016). Clients who suffer from mental health issues such as depression or agoraphobia may become dependent on online interactions, potentially perpetuating their symptoms related to fear of real-life social interactions (Azam, 2017).

### Crises

Counselors who conduct therapy through online sessions have severely limited options in responding to crisis situations; for example, when a therapist suspects suicidal ideation in a client during an online session, direct assistance in implementing a safety plan could not be offered, nor could they escort the client to a clinic (Cherry, 2018; Azam, 2017). It is always possible that a therapist may miss an important text or message for help (Boodman, 2015).

### Maintenance of Therapeutic Relationship

Long-distance therapeutic relationships can be difficult to maintain and research on psychotherapeutic factors has found that the therapeutic relationship is the single most important factor predicting successful outcomes (Azam, 2017). Clinical relationships are centered on the empathic presence of the therapist, the agreement between the therapist and client on tasks and goals, and the building of a bond. Implicit is the importance of social interactions where individuals identify and respond to emotional cues through vocal tones, facial expressions, and body language (Alliant International University, 2019; Cherry, 2018).

Online therapy sessions require therapists and clients to look at their computer screens, not their webcams, minimizing mutual eye contact and losing the important nonverbal cues that give therapists a clear picture of the client's feelings, thoughts, moods, and behaviors (Azam, 2017; Keenan, 2016).

Text-based therapy also completely eliminates non-verbal cues, rendering both clients and therapists with only words on a screen that they must emotionally interpret, leaving room for misinterpretation, placing restrictions on empathic responding, and limiting how well the therapist and client understand each other's personalities and intended meanings (Alliant International University, 2019; Keenan, 2016). Online therapy, in any form, cannot replace the presence of a highly trained, attentive, and compassionate professional that is able to notice a client's behaviors and reactions (Azam, 201).

### Technical Issues

Technical issues and the unreliability of the internet can cause delays or interruptions in the audio and video quality, as well as delivery issues if using text or email, that can undermine the therapeutic experience (Cherry, 2018; Tomikawa, 2017).

### Confidentiality and Privacy

Confidentiality must be kept in online therapy as in more traditional methods of therapy. With the transmission of information online, confidentiality, privacy leaks, and hacking are all of concern (Alliant International University, 2019; Cherry, 2018). Exchanges and texts between the therapist and client can be witnessed and readily accessed by family, friends, and internet hackers (Keenan, 2016).

### Legal and Ethical Rules

While mental health therapy technologies have many advantages, therapists should be aware of the many ethical and legal implications of practicing therapy through technology. Therapists should not only be vigilant regarding any applicable legal and ethical rules, they should gain informed consent and apprise clients of their policies regarding online communication, limits, and boundaries (Armstrong, 2016). Laws such as HIPAA should be at the forefront of any online communication and therapists should take grave care to not inadvertently divulge their client's name, address, phone number, email address, website URL, photograph, and/or anything else that could identify their client (Armstrong, 2016).

**National Board-Certified Counselor Policy (NBCCP)**

In today's technological world, therapists must understand and acknowledge that the nature of the profession is no longer limited to in-person, face-to-face interactions and should consider how their use of technology can be used to better serve their clients (American Counseling Association, 2014). Therapists need to be knowledgeable about online mental health resources as well as to be knowledgeable and understand the additional concerns that technology brings to the field (American Counseling Association, 2014).

The National Board for Certified Counselors (NBCC) (2016) has set forth a policy regarding the provision of distance professional services that supplements the NBCC Code of Ethics and identifies specific actions that nationally certified counselors must take when providing online distance services to clients. These regulations state, in part, that before providing distance services, therapists must review and adhere to all legal regulations from the state in which they and the client are located as well as screen the client for appropriateness to receive distance services in relation to the specific goal (American Counseling Association, 2014; NBCC, 2016).

Therapists must discuss the limitations of confidentiality, privacy concerns, the possibility of technological failure, anticipated response time to electronic communication, and alternate service deliveries (American Counseling Association, 2014; NBCC, 2016). Prior to or during a client's initial session, the therapist shall inform the client of the purposes, goals, procedures, limitations, potential risks, and benefits of online services as well as provide information on rights, responsibilities, privacy, and confidentiality. Therapists should inform clients that due to the ease with which information can inadvertently be shared with others, the therapist must implement methods and behaviors that prevent the distribution of confidential information to unauthorized individuals (American Counseling Association, 2014).

Therapists must avoid the use of public social media sources, such as blogs, to provide confidential information (American Psychological Association, 2014). Instead, therapists must use encryption security for all digital communications therapeutic in nature (NBCC, 2016). To prevent the loss of digital communications or records, secure backup systems must be maintained and if the backup system is also digital in nature, it must have encryption-level security (NBCC, 2016).

Copies should be kept of all written online communications, including email/text messages, instant messages, and histories of chat-based discussions (American Psychological Association, 2014; NBCC, 2016). Records should be maintained for a minimum of five years, unless state laws require additional time, and the use of such records shall be limited to those specifically permitted by law, professional standards, and as specified by agreement with the client (NBCC, 2016)

## Final Thoughts

Although 20% of Americans are diagnosed with a mental illness, mental health provider shortages, finances, stigma, and/or lack of access to care prevent them from receiving adequate treatment. With technological advances, online therapy is now a viable option and opens up therapeutic opportunities for those individuals living in remote areas, that have rigid work schedules, and those whose physical condition or mental health illness make it difficult to travel.

Cognitive and behavioral techniques used in more traditional types of therapy can now be incorporated online through the use of education, skills training, activities, and exercises with structured content being delivered via text, pictures, animations, audio files, and videos that can be completed by the client anytime, anywhere.

With more than 10,000 mental health applications to carefully choose from, an individual's phone can be transformed into a therapeutic program capable of attaining real-time mental health symptoms and delivering immediate therapy; therefore, improving treatment outcomes for some mental health disorders. Online tools such as blogs, can also help educate our society on a variety of mental health conditions in hopes to stop the stigma surrounding mental illness.

## Points to Remember

- *Online therapy may broaden communication between a therapist and client but raises issues of unclear boundaries, limits of confidentiality, ambiguity, inappropriate expectations, and limited options in crisis situations.*
- *The therapeutic relationship is the single most important factor in predicting successful therapy outcomes due to the empathetic presence of the therapist, social interactions*

*between therapist and client, and the emotional cues garnered from facial expressions, body language, and tone of voice. Online therapy sessions can minimize and even lose these important emotional cues that help therapists understand their client's feelings, thoughts, moods, and behaviors.*
- *Therapy via text limits the therapist and client from understanding each other and their intended meanings.*
- *Individuals using online therapy and treatments to supplement traditional modes of therapy are more likely to remain engaged in face-to-face therapy.*
- *Despite the prevalence of mental health apps, there is no evidence they are evidence-based or effective and some have even been identified as harmful and dangerous.*
- *Therapists providing therapy through technology must adhere to all legal regulations and discuss with their clients the limitations of confidentiality, privacy concerns, the possibility of technological failure, anticipated response time to electronic communication, and alternate service deliveries.*

# Chapter Ten

# Professional Resources for Counselors: Organizations and EBP Resources

Just like any vocation, mental health professionals are faced with unique demands that they must care for in order to be at their best for their clients. Stressors on therapists can include emotional, physical, and legal issues that can quickly become intensified if not dealt with properly. The stress of helping patients through some of their most intense challenges can take its toll on the therapist's emotional well-being. Therapists in private practice may feel as though they are alone in their profession with limited options for networking.

There are, however, many professional organizations that provide support to counselors, both through access to resources and to a community of other therapists treating similar groups of patients or using similar modalities of treatment. Many of these organizations provide free access to research-based resources and interventions, helping counselors to remain abreast of the latest innovations in the field. Other organizations charge a fee for admission but provide discounted wellness benefits and training opportunities for members. This chapter provides an overview of some of these organizations along with their direct links; which were accurate at the time of publishing. An overview of evidence-based practice sites is also provided to help therapists locate more information about EBPs for consideration in practice.

## Professional Organizations

### American Mental Health Counselors Association (AMHCA)

As the leading national organization for licensed mental health counselors, AMHCA provides counselors with advocacy, leadership, and professional collaboration. This association is dedicated to providing the most up-to-date resources for counselors in practice. Counselors who join the AMHCA can enjoy such benefits as members-only low rate professional liability insurance, continuing education opportunities, professional networking opportunities, and access to the *Journal of Mental Health Counseling*. As a member, counselors also have access to an online community in which they can join in discussion or post topics. This is especially helpful for counselors who may be practicing individually and need to bounce an idea off a professional colleague.

For students, the AMHCA offers discounted membership rates that include discounts toward the AMHCA Annual Conference. Students who are in either a masters or doctoral degree program are eligible for the student membership. The AMHCA highly recommends student participation as it provides future practitioners with access to networking opportunities, as well as helping students to become involved in advocating for patients' rights.

In addition to the online resources, the AMHCA holds an annual conference where professionals can connect face-to-face with others from the field, as well as to attend workshops presented by experts in the mental health profession. The conference is a 3-day affair in which attendees can acquire continuing education credits toward their license renewal requirements. More information on AMHCA can be found at www.amhca.org

**American Counseling Association (ACA)**

The ACA is the world's largest non-profit, professional counseling organization. They are dedicated to seeing mental health professionals grow within their practice through continued education and support. The ACA was founded in 1952 with the purpose of representing mental health professionals in a multitude of settings. Since then, the ACA has continually promoted the professional development of counselors, advocated for the profession, and supported ethical standards in the mental health field.

According to the ACA's strategic plan, the association's core values include diversity, equity, inclusion, integrity, proactive leadership, professional relations, scientific knowledge, and social justice. Their mission is to promote these core values through connecting professionals to evidence-based resources and to each other. The ACA looks at the counselor holistically and works to ensure overall wellness and support within the profession.

Counselors can obtain a paid membership with the ACA. There are a variety of membership levels in the ACA – students, counselors without a master's degree, counselors with master's degrees and above, and retired counselors. Each tier of membership includes specific benefits for the member, including access to the *Journal of Counseling and Development* and *Counseling Today*, tools for complying with ethical standards, and free annual online courses for professional development. For more information on ACA, visit https://www.counseling.org

**International Association of Marriage and Family Counselors (IAMFC)**

The IAMFC is a division of the ACA and was created to help connect marriage and family therapists with others in the mental health profession. The IAMFC's goals include providing a therapist-driven forum for exploring marital and family issues, connecting diverse groups of professionals, and promoting collaborative efforts in the field of marriage and family therapy. Like other organizations, membership includes access to professional journals, as well as opportunities for networking with other professionals. The IAMFC also provides family therapy certification opportunities through the National Credentialing Academy.

The IAMFC holds an annual world conference in which attendees can participate in presentations and workshops designed to further education and best practices in the field of marital and family therapy. Participants can gain credits for continuing education toward license requirements and can enjoy a diversity of research and practice topics presented by top practitioners in the field. For more information on all of the benefits and resources available to members, please visit www.iamfconline.org

**Association for Specialists in Group Work (ASGW)**

The ASGW is a division of the ACA created to assist practitioners with practicing effective and ethical group work with clients. The ASGW focuses on providing members with resources on the best ways in which to work with groups of diverse individuals who are dealing with complex mental health issues. Their goal is to create a community in which professionals can seek leadership as well as professional and personal development opportunities, which supports the increasingly burgeoning community of mental health professionals who provide group therapy treatment.

In addition to the standard membership benefits of joining an organization, the ASGW provides members with evidence-based practices and innovative models for working in group therapy sessions. The ASGW also focuses on inclusivity and multiculturalism in the promotion of socially just practices in the group model. Membership is not only available to professionals practicing group therapy, but also to others with an interest in this modality, such as general social workers and therapists who treat individuals. For more information on ASGW, visit https://asgw.org

## American Association for Marriage and Family Therapy (AAMFT)

The AAMFT is a professional organization that represents over 50,000 marriage and family therapists in the United States, Canada, and abroad. Founded in 1942, the AAMFT seeks to assist marriage and family therapists with understanding the needs of couples and familial relationships. The AAMFT provides therapists with resources on ethical treatment standards, training, and licensing opportunities. The AAMFT develops standards for graduate education and training, along with clinical supervision, professional ethics, and clinical practice. The AAMFT is also responsible for publishing the *Journal of Marital and Family Therapy*.

Similar to other professional organizations, members can enjoy benefits such as discounts on professional liability insurance, access to journals and newsletters, discounted continuing education credits, and legal and ethical consultation. The AAMFT recommends vendors that can provide members with additional services from discounted directory listings in *Psychology Today* to credit card processing solutions. The AAMFT also helps with employee recruitment in order to help practitioners expand their practices and find qualified professionals across the country. For more information on AAMFT, visit https://www.aamft.org

## American School Counselors Association (ASCA)

School counselors are an integral part of the professional counseling network, and they provide school-based mental health services to a population that includes the most vulnerable individuals – children. Although school counselors aren't tasked with providing clinical-based services to students, they are often exposed to the same level of critical issues as clinical practitioners. School counselors must be able to work with community-based mental health services, private therapists, and oftentimes state agencies in order to help students gain access to appropriate mental health services. School counselors must help students to navigate the school system as a whole, including academics, peer relations, and transitional, post-secondary services.

Organizations such as ASCA support school counselors in their efforts to help students find success in all aspects of school-based life. They are focused on providing school counselors with professional development assistance and other resources that will allow them to help students fulfill their goals through education and mental health support. Membership in ASCA provides school counselors with continued support with the latest research and trends, evidence-based practices for increasing student success, and professional development opportunities to help with continuing certification. More information on ASCA can be found at https://www.schoolcounselor.org

**Other Professional Organizations for Specific Practice Areas**

The following is not an exhaustive list of organizations for specific practice areas; rather, it provides a jumping-off point for counselors looking to gain more information for very specific groups of patients:

- Association for Creativity in Counseling (ACC) http://www.creativecounselor.org
- Association for Adult Development and Aging (AADA) http://www.aadaweb.org
- American College Counseling Association (ACCA) http://collegecounseling.org
- Association for Counselors and Educators in Government (ACEG) http://www.acegonline.org
- Association for Lesbian, Gay, Bisexual, and Transgender Issues in Counseling (ALGBTIC) http://algbtic.org
- The Association for Humanistic Counseling (AHC) http://afhc.camp9.org
- Association for Spiritual, Ethical, and Religious Values in Counseling (ASERVIC) http://www.aservic.org
- International Association of Addiction and Offender Counselors (IAAOC) http://www.iaaoc.org
- National Employment Counseling Association (NEC) http://www.employmentcounseling.org

## Resources for Evidence-Based Practices (EBP)

**Group Therapy**

**Seeking Safety:** Seeking Safety is an evidence-based program designed to improve the treatment outcomes for patients suffering from trauma and substance abuse disorder. The program consists of 25 session topics that can be adapted to fit a variety of group profiles. The goal of the Seeking Safety program is to help patients attain safety in their interpersonal relationships as well as within their own thought patterns. To accomplish this, the program integrates treatment for both trauma and substance abuse, focuses on counteracting negative thought patterns, and gives special attention to the patient's emotional responses to treatment and progress. For more information on the program overview and training options, please visit https://www.treatment-innovations.org

**Mindfulness-Based Relapse Prevention (MBRP):** MBRP is a program based on the integration of mindfulness and cognitive behavioral relapse prevention. The goal of the program is to teach patients ways in which to stop their automatic reactions to situations in favor of acknowledging their feelings and thinking through better ways of handling issues with the goal of preventing relapse into substance abuse or other negative behaviors. Although MBRP can be practiced in a multitude of settings, it has shown positive results as a group therapy method in reducing the likelihood of relapse in patients who participate even sporadically in treatment.

There are a number of websites that provide resources for practitioners interested in MBRP.

- The developers of the program, who continue to provide training in MBRP, can be found at http://www.mindfulrp.com.
- The American Addiction Center is another resource for MBRP, and they provide information on utilizing MBRP in a 12-step recovery program. They can be found at https://www.mentalhelp.net.
- For counselors interested in the latest research surrounding MBRP, the National Center for Biotechnology Information, a division of the National Institutes of Health, provides numerous scholarly articles on the subject. For more information, visit www.ncbi.nih.gov.

### Individual Therapy

**Dialectical Behavior Therapy (DBT):** For practitioners working with individual clients using DBT, there are several digital resources available, although it is important to note that as with all digital resources, individuals must be discerning of their validity. The National Institutes of Health offer scholarly articles on DBT in practice as well as research in the field. For more of an overview of DBT along with videos of treatment options, Behavioral Tech is a resource that provides a wide variety of information to both therapists and the general community. Founded in 2002 as a division of the Linehan Institute, Behavioral Tech aims to provide training to practitioners based on evidence-backed research. For more information, visit https://behavioraltech.org.

For therapists who are looking for more general information on DBT that can be adapted within their practice, the Positive Psychology Program offers blog-style information on DBT as well as worksheets that therapists can use with clients in practice. DBT is not the only treatment option offered through this resource, so practitioners who are using other types of treatment may find this site to be quite helpful for other areas of practice. For more information, please visit https://positivepsychologyprogram.com/category/therapies/.

**Mindfulness-Based Cognitive Therapy (MBCT):** MBCT is centered on the mindfulness-based stress reduction program developed by Jon Kabat-Zinn. Research suggests that mindfulness-based stress reduction can help with chronic pain and other health problems, as well as psychological disorders such as anxiety and depression. MBCT combines the principles from Kabat-Zinn's program with theories from cognitive behavior therapy to develop a program that would work specifically with individuals who suffer from depression. For an overview of MCBT along with access to TED talks, book suggestions, community resources, and training options, please visit http://www.mbct.com/index.html. For current articles on MBCT, *Psychology Today* offers subscribers with access to past and current research in the field. Subscribers can also link to therapists who practice MBCT in their area. For more information, visit https://www.psychologytoday.com/us/therapy-types/mindfulness-based-cognitive-therapy.

**Exposure Therapy:** While there aren't many digital resources that deal primarily with exposure therapy in practice, the American Psychological Association (APA) offers an overview of exposure therapy, mainly for patients, including which disorders exposure therapy has been scientifically proven to be successful in treating. The APA also provides an overview of the types of exposure therapy that can be used depending on the severity of need and the amount of exposure needed. For more information about exposure therapy, visit https://www.apa.org/ptsd-guideline/patients-and-families/exposure-therapy. For information about exposure therapy geared toward practitioners, scholarly journals are the most valid places to search for information. Publications such as the *Journal of the American Medical Association* and the *Journal of Psychiatric Research* can be invaluable resources for the most up-to-date research in the area of exposure therapies.

## Family Therapy

**Ecologically-Based Family Therapy (EBFT):** Targeting families with adolescents who abuse substances and/or are runaways, EBFT aims to address the immediate treatment needs of adolescents and their families in order to resolve runaway behaviors and to facilitate an emotional reconnection to the family through increased communication and problem-solving skills. Therapy focuses on environmental factors that impact familial relationships. The program focuses on both the adolescent and the parent/caregiver in order to increase coping skills for both family members.

The California Evidence-Based Clearinghouse for Child Welfare (CEBC) has extensive information on EBFT, including an overview of the target population and program, goals, components of the program, training, research and additional resources for practitioners. For more information, visit http://www.cebc4cw.org/program/ecologically-based-family-therapy/

**Brief Strategic Family Therapy (BSFT):** Developed at the University of Miami's Center for Family Studies, BSFT focuses on changing patterns of family interaction that encourage problematic adolescent behavior. The treatment is designed to be a short-term intervention. The National Institutes of Health provide several scholarly articles discussing the BFST model, as well as research studies with treatment outcomes. The Brief Strategic Family Therapy Institute at the University of Miami Center for Family Studies can provide further information about the development of the BFST intervention. For more information, visit
https://www.publichealth.med.miami.edu/research/research-centers/brief-strategic-family-therapy-bsft-institute/index.html.

**Family Centered Treatment (FCT):** FCT integrates two different models of family therapy, Emotionally Focused Therapy and Eco-Structural Family Therapy. FCT is also influenced by a peer-helping-peer model that increases effective communication and engagement among family members. FCT is based on best practice standards that include delivering intervention in the client's home, utilizing flexible hours and 24-hour access to crisis intervention, and the use of a variety of research-based interventions. The Family Centered Treatment Foundation provides extensive information on providing FCT within a variety of family structures. For more information, visit
http://www.familycenteredtreatment.org/the-fct-model.

## Couples Therapy

**Gottman Method:** One of the two most widely practiced couples therapy treatment interventions, the Gottman Method has been extensively researched. In summary, the Gottman Method focuses on resolving conflicts within relationships when it may feel as though a solution cannot be discovered. An emphasis is placed on increasing respect and closeness within the relationship, in addition to learning how to handle conflict constructively in order to preserve the relationship. For more information on the Gottman Method, visit The Gottman Institute at https://www.gottman.com.

**Emotionally Focused Couples Therapy (EFT):** This model uses the science of adult attachment and bonding to treat couples who are in conflict. EFT focuses on replacing previous negative behaviors that lead to problems in communication with positive behaviors that allow couples to open up and learn from each other. The practitioner examines patterns of behavior within the relationship and uses that evidence to diffuse problematic interpersonal behaviors. For more information on EFT, visit the International Centre for Excellence in Emotionally Focused Therapy at https://iceeft.com/what-is-eft/.

### E-Therapy

As a relatively new practice over the past two decades, e-therapy, which encompasses tele-counseling, video chat, and other forms of virtual interaction, can be beneficial for clients who are looking for a more time- and cost-effective method of receiving mental health services. There are many digital resources for this type of therapy, depending on the desired outcome for the client. According to TalkSpace, an online application for e-therapy, clients are assessed and are paired with a therapist that matches their unique needs. TalkSpace provides e-therapy for multiple modalities, including individual and couples, and also has therapy options for teens. Payment options are available depending upon the level of service needed. TalkSpace combines text messaging and video chatting as a means of providing on-demand therapeutic intervention. For more information, visit https://www.talkspace.com.

Other e-therapy programs provide various virtual options for connecting with therapists. The programs also boast that they are HIPAA compliant with licensed therapists who can fit a variety of needs. To find out more about services offered by these companies, visit the following sites:

- BetterHelp: provides access to counselors with a wide range of specialties: www.betterhelp.com
- ReGain: specializes in relationship counseling: www.regain.us
- MyTherapist: provides access to counselors with a wide range of specialties: www.mytherapist.com
- BreakThrough: provides access to counselors with a wide range of specialties: www.breakthrough.com

There are also a myriad of other applications that offer basic chat and discussion boards, as well as more intensive assistance. Depending upon the application, a fee may be charged, but there are many that are free. The following is a listing of some popular e-therapy applications that can be downloaded onto smartphones and tablets. These can be searched wherever apps are downloaded dependent upon the smartphone platform:

- 7 Cups (Anxiety and stress chat)
- Youper (Anxiety and depression help through artificial intelligence)
- Couples Therapy (Relationship counseling app)
- Wysa (Stress, depression, and anxiety therapy through chat)
- Online Counseling (Depression and anxiety therapy)
- Pride Counseling (LGBT-specialized therapy)
- Headspace (Meditation training)

# Acronyms

| | |
|---|---|
| ADHD | Attention Deficit/Hyperactivity Disorder: A chronic condition whose symptoms include a lack of ability to focus on a particular task for any length of time as well as having signs of hyperactivity and sometimes being impulsive. |
| AMCD | Association for Multicultural Counseling and Development: Organization that provides specific competencies for therapists when working with diverse clients. |
| APA | American Psychiatric Association |
| BD | Behavior Disorder: one of several anxiety disorders |
| BPD | Borderline Personality Disorder: a disorder characterized by impairments in empathy, intimacy, self-direction, and self-image, as well as emotional liability, anxiety, and separation insecurity. |
| BSFT | Brief Strategic Family Therapy: a form of therapy that focuses on adolescent substance abuse using a manualized system. |
| CBT | Cognitive Behavior Therapy: a form of therapy that aims to reframe negative thought patterns and subsequent behaviors. |
| DBT | Dialectical Behavior Therapy: a form of therapy that combines classical and operant conditioning through the analysis of behavior. |
| EBP | Evidence-Based Practices: The integration of clinical expertise, research, and patient values that provide therapeutic practices from therapist to patients in need of assistance. |
| EEFT | Emotionally-Focused Family Therapy: Therapy that focuses on increasing family members' abilities to help promote mental health recovery in their loved ones rather than problem-solving. |
| EFT | Emotionally Focused Couples' Therapy: attachment-based therapy approach that is used with couples in which one partner has depression, chronic illness, or post-traumatic stress disorders. |
| FFT | Functional Family Therapy: Short-term therapy based on a manualized system that targets children and adolescents who exhibit problems with juvenile delinquency, substance abuse, |

and violent tendencies.

HIPAA — Health Insurance Portability and Accountability Act of 1996: U.S. legislation that provides security and privacy for personal medical information.

iCBT — Online Cognitive Behavioral Therapy: Using traditional CBT in an online format that may include video chat, text, email, audio files, pictures or animations.

MBCT — Mindfulness-Based Cognitive Therapy: a form of therapy that combines mindfulness practices with elements of CBT.

MBRP — Mindfulness-Based Relapse Prevention: an intervention that combines mindfulness practices with coping strategies.

NBCC — National Board for Certified Counselors: and international organizations that supports certified counselors.

OCD — Obsessive Compulsive Disorder: one of several anxiety disorders

PTSD — Post-Traumatic Stress Disorder: one of several anxiety disorders

SFBT — Solution-Focused Brief Therapy: used to find a quick solution to an issue while working towards a more secure future. May be used with other therapy styles.

# References

Abrams, R., & Penn, P. (N.D.). *Mindfulness-based relapse preventions for addictive behaviors: An evidence-based group approach.* Arizona State University. Retrieved from https://cabhp.asu.edu/sites/default/files/session-19-mindfulness-based-relapse-prevention-an-evidenced-based-.pdf

Ackerman, C. (2019a). *What is family therapy? +6 techniques and interventions.* Retrieved from https://positivepsychologyprogram.com/family-therapy/

Ackerman, C. (2019b). *Emotion focused therapy: Understanding emotions to improve relationships.* Retrieved from https://positivepsychologyprogram.com/emotion-focused-therapy/

Ackerman, C. (2018). *What is solution-focused therapy: 3 essential techniques.* Retrieved from https://positivepsychologyprogram.com/solution-focused-therapy/

Adi, R., Pagel, M.J., Whitaker, J., & Urbanek, A.P. (2019). *The real crisis in mental health today.* Retrieved from https://www.cchr.org/cchr-reports/the-real-crisis/introduction.html

Alexander, J.F., Waldron, H.B., Robbins, M.S., & Neeb, A.A. (2013). *Functional family therapy for adolescent behavior problems.* Arlington, VA: American Psychological Association.

Alliant International University. (2019). *Is it the right time to begin using technology in your counseling?* Retrieved from https://www.alliant.edu/blog/right-time-begin-using-technology-counseling/

Altamarino, N., & Chandler, D. (2013). *Is a non-traditional family structure completely doomed for failure?* Retrieved from https://my.vanderbilt.edu/developmentalpsychologyblog/2013/12/is-a-non-traditional-family-structure-completely-doomed-for-failure-how-you-can-make-sure-your-child-thrives-despite-the-odds/

American Counseling Association. (2014). *2014 ACA Code of Ethics.* Retrieved from https://www.counseling.org/resources/aca-code-of-ethics.pdf

American Psychological Association. (2005). *Report of the 2005 presidential task force on evidence-based practice.* Retrieved from https://www.apa.org/practice/resources/evidence/evidence-based-report.pdf

American Psychiatric Association. (2013). *Diagnostic and statistical manual of mental disorders* (5th ed.). Arlington, VA: American Psychiatric Publishing.

American Psychological Association. (2019). *Guidelines for assessment of and intervention with persons with disabilities.* Retrieved from https://www.apa.org/pi/disability/resources/assessment-disabilities

American Psychological Association. (2018). *App evaluation model.* Retrieved from https://www.psychiatry.org/psychiatrists/practice/mental-health-apps/app-evaluation-model

American Psychological Association. (n.d.). *What is exposure therapy?* Retrieved from https://www.div12.org/sites/default/files/WhatIsExposureTherapy.pdf

American Psychological Association. (2012). Guidelines for psychological practice with lesbian, gay, and bisexual clients. *American Psychologist, 67*(1), 10-42. DOI: 10.1037/a0024659

American Psychological Association. (2019a). *Psychotherapy: Understanding group therapy.* Retrieved from https://www.apa.org/helpcenter/group-therapy

American Psychological Association. (2019b). *Clinical guideline for the treatment of posttraumatic stress disorder: What is exposure therapy?* Retrieved from https://www.apa.org/ptsd-guideline/patients-and-families/exposure-therapy

Armstrong, B. (2016). *The legalities and ethics of texting your psychotherapy clients.* Retrieved from https://therapymarketinginstitute.com/legalities-ethics-texting-psychotherapy-clients/?doing_wp_cron=1550263268.1418390274047851562500

Anderson, M. & Cardoza, K. (2016). A silent epidemic. *NPR.* Retrieved from http://apps.npr.org/mental-health/

Antin, L. (2018). *Solution-focused brief therapy (SFBT).* Retrieved from https://www.goodtherapy.org/learn-about-therapy/types/solution-focused-therapy

Arredondo, P., Toporek, M. S., Brown, S., Jones, J., Locke, D. C., Sanchez, J. & Stadler, H. (1996) Operationalization of the Multicultural Counseling Competencies. Alexandria, VA: AMCD

Azam, A. (2017). *Pros and cons of online therapy: Are we hard-wired to connect? Retrieved* from http://blog.time2track.com/pros-and-cons-of-online-therapy-are-we-hard-wired-to-connect

Baldwin, S.A., Christian, S., Berkeljon, A., & Shadish, W.R. (2012). The effects of family therapies for adolescent delinquency and substance abuse: A meta-analysis. *Journal of Marital and Family Therapy, 38*(1), 281-304. DOI: 10.1111/j.1752-0606.2011.00248.x

Barends, E.G.R., & Briner, R.B. (2014). Teaching evidence-based practice: Lessons from the pioneers. An interview with Amanda Burls and Gordon Guyatt. *Academy of Management & Education, 13*(3), 476-483. DOI: 10.5465/amle.2014.0136

# References

Barlow, S. H., Fuhriman, A. J., & Burlingame, G. M. (2004). The History of Group Counseling and Psychotherapy. In J. L. DeLucia-Waack, D. A. Gerrity, C. R. Kalodner, & M. T. Riva (Eds.), *Handbook of group counseling and psychotherapy* (pp. 3-22). Thousand Oaks, CA: Sage Publications Ltd.

Beasley, N. (2019). Therapy and counseling: A new age of technology approaches. Retrieved from https://www.betterhelp.com/advice/therapy/therapy-and-counseling-a-new-age-of-technology-approaches/

Benjamin, C.L., Puleo, C.M., Settipani, C.A., Brodman, D.M., Edmunds, J.M., Cummings, C.M., & Kendall, P.C. (2011). History of cognitive-behavioral therapy (CBT) in youth. *Child and Adolescent Psychiatric Clinics of North America, 20*(2), 179-189. DOI: 10.1016/j.chc.2011.01.011

Boodman, E. (2015). *Psychotherapy by emoji: Mental health community wrestles with texting.* Retrieved from https://www.statnews.com/2015/11/30/psychotherapy-texting-mental-health/

Bowen, S., Chawla, N. & Marlatt, G.A. (2010). *Mindfulness-based relapse prevention for addictive behaviors: A clinician's guide.* New York, NY: Guilford Press

Brady, V.P. & Whitman, S.M. (2011). An acceptance and mindfulness-based approach to social phobia: A case study. *Journal of College Counseling, 15*(1),81-96. DOI: 10.1002/j.2161-1882.2012.00007.x

Bussing-Birks, M. (2019). *Mental illness and substance abuse.* Retrieved from https://www.nber.org/digest/apr02/w8699.html

California State University Channel Islands [CSUCI]. (2019). *Individual counseling.* Retrieved from https://www.csuci.edu/caps/individual-counseling.htm

Centers for Disease Control and Prevention. (2018). *Learn about mental health: Mental health basics. Retrieved* from https://www.cdc.gov/mentalhealth/learn/index.htm

Chapman, A.L. (2006). Dialectical behavior therapy: Current indications and unique elements. *Psychiatry, 3*(9), 62-68. Retrieved from https://www.ncbi.nlm.nih.gov/pmc/articles/PMC2963469/

Chapman, B.P., Talbot, N., Tatman, A.W., & Brition, P.C. (2009). Personality traits and the Working alliance in psychotherapy trainees: An organizing role for the five factor model? *Journal of Social and Clinical Psychology, 28*(5). DOI: 10.1521/jscp.2009.28.5.577

Cheang, J. and Doshi, S. (2017). *How a video game could change the way we think about mental health.* Retrieved from https://www.mentalhealthamerica.net/blog/how-video-game-could-change-way-we-think-about-mental-health

Chen-Ling, L. & Yun, W. (2016). Client motivation: An integration of theory and practice in counseling and psychotherapy. *Advances in Psychological Science, 24*(2), 261-269. DOI: 10.3724/SP.J.1042.2016.00261

Cherry, K. (2018). *Advantages and disadvantages of online therapy.* Retrieved from https://www.verywellmind.com/advantages-and-disadvantages-of-online-therapy-2795225

Chung, B., Mikesell, L. & Miklowitz, D. (2014). Flexibility and structure may enhance implementation of family-focused therapy in community mental health settings. *Community Mental Health Journal, 50*(7), 878-791. DOI: 10.1007/s10597-014-9733-8

Colangelo, I. (2015). *Everything you need to know about couples therapy.* Retrieved from https://www.talkspace.com/blog/2015/02/everything-you-need-to-know-about-couples-therapy/

Commonwealth of Virginia: Commission on Youth. (2017). *Collection of evidence-based practices for children and adolescents with mental health treatment needs.* Retrieved from http://vcoy.virginia.gov/documents/collection/Collection2017online.pdf

Cook, S.C., Schwartz, A.C., & Kaslow, N.J. (2017). Evidence-based psychotherapy: Advantages and challenges. *Neurotherapeutics, 14*(3), 537-545. DOI: 10.1007/s13311-017-0549-4

Cox, M.L. (2017). The role of the therapeutic alliance on the successful outcome of transfers in marriage and family therapy cases. Retrieved from https://scholarsarchive.byu.edu/cgi/viewcontent.cgi?article=7517&context=etd

Cully, J.A., & Teten, A.L. (2008). A therapist's guide to brief cognitive behavioral therapy. Department of Veterans Affairs South Central MIRECC, Houston. Retrieved from https://www.mirecc.va.gov/visn16/docs/therapists_guide_to_brief_cbtmanual.pdf

Cunningham, P. (2009). Beyond parity: Primary care physicians' perspectives on access to mental health care. Health Affairs, 28, 490-501. DOI: 10.1377/hlthaff.28.3.w490

Curry, S., Marlatt, G.A., & Gordon, J.R. (1987). Abstinence violation effect: Validation of an attributional construct with smoking cessation. *Journal of Consulting and Clinical Psychology, 55*(2), 145-149. DOI: 10.1037/0022-006X.55.2.145

Dashnaw, D. (2017). *Attachment theory and couples therapy.* Retrieved from https://couplestherapyinc.com/attachment-theory/

Datchi, C.C., & Sexton, T.L. (2013). Can family therapy have an effect on adult criminal conduct? Initial evaluation of functional family therapy. *Couple and Family Psychology: Research and Practice, 2*(4), 278-293 DOI: 10.1037/a0034166

Dolan, Y. (2017). *What is solution-focused therapy?* Retrieved from https://solutionfocused.net/what-is-solution-focused-therapy/

Dore, J. (2016). *Five tips for multicultural competence in counseling.* Retrieved from https://pro.psychcentral.com/five-tips-for-multicultural-competence-in-therapy/

Dutch, D. (2019). *Is therapeutic alliance the foundation of counselling.* Retrieved from http://eac.eu.com/publications/therapeutic-alliance/

E-Counseling. (2019). Best online therapy services compared – April 2019. Retrieved from https://www.e-counseling.com/online-therapy/

Eagan, K., Stolzenberg, E.B., Zimmerman, H.B., Aragon, M.C., Sayson, H.W. & Rios-Aguilar, C. (2017). *The American freshman: National norms fall 2016.* Retrieved from https://www.heri.ucla.edu/monographs/TheAmericanFreshman2016.pdf

Edwards-Tate, L. (2018). *Mental illness on the rise in America.* Retrieved from https://www.commdiginews.com/health-science/health/mental-illness-on-the-rise-in-america-107580/

Eisendrath, S., Chartier, M., & McLane, M. (2011). Adapting mindfulness-based cognitive therapy for treatment-resistant depression. *Cognitive and Behavioral Practice, 18,* 263-370. DOI: 10.106/j.cbpra.2010.05.004

Elkins, D. (2015). *The 5 qualities that tell you a therapist is effective.* Retrieved from https://www.psychologytoday.com/us/blog/the-human-dimension/201511/the-5-qualities-tell-you-therapist-is-effective

Emmelkamp, P.M., David, D., Beckers, T., Muris, P., Cuijpers, P., Lutz, W., ... & Vervliet, B. (2014). Advancing psychotherapy and evidence-based psychological interventions. *International Journal of Methods in Psychiatric Research, 23*(1), 58-91. DOI: 10.1002/mpr.1411

Encyclopaedia Britannica. (2019). Group therapy. Retrieved from https://www.britannica.com/topic/group-therapy

Estes, J. (2017). *What to consider when working with underserved populations.* Retrieved from https://thesandiegopsychologist.com/2017/06/30/what-to-consider-when-working-with-underserved-populations/

Felmingham, K.L., & Bryant, R.A. (2012). Gender differences in the maintenance of response to cognitive behavior therapy for posttraumatic stress disorder. *Journal of Consulting and Clinical Psychology, 80*(2), 196-200. DOI: 10.1037/a0027156

Feuerman, M. (2019). *Your attachment style influences the success of your relationship.* Retrieved from https://www.gottman.com/blog/attachment-style-influences-success-relationship/

Filges, T., Andersen, D., & Klint Jorgensen, A.M. (2018). Functional family therapy for young people in treatment for nonopioid drug use: A systematic review. *Journal of Social Work Practice, 28*(2), 131-145. DOI: 10.1177/1049731516629802

Firestone, L. (2016). *The importance of relationship in therapy: How a strong therapeutic alliance can lead to real change.* Retrieved from https://www.psychologytoday.com/us/blog/compassion-matters/201612/the-importance-the-relationship-in-therapy

Firestone, R. (2019). *Qualities of an ideal therapist.* Retrieved from https://www.psychalive.org/qualities-of-an-ideal-therapist/

Foa, E.B. & McLean, C.P. (2016). The efficacy of exposure therapy for anxiety-related disorders and its underlying mechanisms: The case of OCD and PTSD. *Annual Review of Clinical Psychology, 12,* 1-28. DOI: 10.1146/annurev-clinpsy-021815-093533

Foroughe, M., Stillar, A., Goldstein, L., Dolhanty, J., Goodcase, E. T., & Lafrance, A. (2018). Brief emotion-focused family therapy: An intervention for parents of children and adolescents with mental health issues. *Journal of Marital and Family Therapy.* DOI: 10.1111/jmft.12351

Fox, M. (2018). *Major depression on the rise among everyone, new data shows: Biggest increase in diagnoses in teens.* Retrieved from https://www.nbcnews.com/health/health-news/major-depression-rise-among-everyone-new-data-shows-n873146

France, D. (2017). *8 things a veteran wants their mental health counselor to know.* Retrieved from https://www.brainline.org/blog/head-space-and-timing/8-things-veteran-wants-their-mental-health-counselor-know

Fuertes, J.N., Bady-Amoon, P., Thind, N., & Chang, T. (2015). The therapy relationship in multicultural psychotherapy. *Psychotherapy Bulletin, 50*(1), 41-45. Retrieved from https://societyforpsychotherapy.org/the-therapy-relationship-in-multicultural-psychotherapy/

Gehart, D.R. (2012). The mental health recovery movement and family therapy, part 1: Consumer-led reform of services to persons diagnosed with severe mental illness. *Journal of Marital and Family Therapy, 38*(3), 429-439. DOI: 10.1111/j.1752.0606.2011.00230.x

Ghee, A.C., Bolling, L.C., & Johnson, C.S. (2009). The efficacy of a condensed seeking safety intervention for women in residential chemical dependence treatment at 30 days posttreatment. *Journal of Child Sexual Abuse, 18*(5), 475-488. DOI: 10.1080/10538710903183287

Ginicola, M. (2014). Culture corner – Counselor know thyself: Developing self-awareness within the multicultural competence counseling model. *Connecticut Counseling Association.* Retrieved from https://ccacounseling.com/culture-corner-counselor-know-thyself-developing-self-awareness-within-the-multicultural-competence-counseling-model/

Gleit, L. (2017). *The role of telemedicine in mental health.* Retrieved from https://www.healthitoutcomes.com/doc/the-role-of-telemedicine-in-mental-health-0001

Good Therapy. (2018). *Emotionally focused therapy.* Retrieved from https://www.goodtherapy.org/learn-about-therapy/types/emotionally-focused-therapy

Gottman, J. (2015). *The empirical basis for Gottman Method couples therapy.* Retrieved from https://www.gottman.com/blog/the-empirical-basis-for-gottman-method-couples-therapy/

Green, S.M., & Bieling, P.J. (2012). Expanding the scope of mindfulness-based cognitive therapy: Evidence for effectiveness in a heterogeneous psychiatric sample. *Cognitive and Behavioral Practice, 19*(1), 174-180. DOI: 10.1016/j.cbpra.2011.02.006

Greenhalgh, T., Howick, J., & Maskrey, N. (2014). Evidence-based medicine: A movement in crisis? *British Medical Journal, 14*(3), 537-545. DOI: 10.1007/s13311-017-0549-4

Groth-Marnet, G., Roberts, R., & Beutler, L.E. (2001). Client characteristics and psychotherapy: Perspectives, support, interactions, and implications for training. *Australian Psychologist, 36*(2), 115-121. DOI: 10.1080/000500601082596643

Gunderson, J.G., Daversa, M.T., Grilo, C.M., McGlashan, T.H., Zanarini, M.C., Shea, M.T., ... & Stout, R.L. (2006). Predictors of 2-year outcomes

for patients with borderline Personality disorder. *American Journal of Psychiatry, 163*(5), 822-826.
DOI: 10.1176/ajp.2006.163.5.822

Gurton, A. (2019). *Understanding the therapeutic alliance.* Retrieved from https://www.mentalhelp.net/blogs/understanding-the-therapeutic-alliance/

Harper, S.K., Webb, T.L., & Rayner, K. (2013). The effectiveness of mindfulness-based interventions for supporting people with intellectual disabilities: A narrative review. *Behavior Modification, 37*(3), 431-453. DOI: 10.1177/01455445513476085

Hawley, L.D., Leibert, T.W., & Lane, J.A. (2017). *The relationship between socioeconomic status and counseling outcomes.* Retrieved from http://tpcjournal.nbcc.org/the-relationship-between-socioeconomic-status-and-counseling-outcomes/

Hebert, M., & Bergeron, M. (2007). Efficacy of a group intervention for adult women survivors of sexual abuse. *Journal of Child Sexual Abuse, 16*(4), 37-61. DOI: 10.1300/J070v16n04_03

Henriques, G. (2014). *The college student mental health crisis.* Retrieved from https://www.psychologytoday.com/us/blog/theory-knowledge/201402/the-college-student-mental-health-crisis

Hien, D.A., Morgan-Lopez, A.A., Campbell, A.N.C., Saavedra, L.M., Wu, E., Cohen, L., ... & Nunes, E.V. (2012). Attendance and substance use outcomes for the seeking safety program: Sometimes less is more. *Journal of Counseling and Clinical Psychology, 80*(1), 29-42. DOI: 10.1037/a0026361

Higgins, E. (2017). *Is mental health declining in the U.S.?* Retrieved from https://www.scientificamerican.com/article/is-mental-health-declining-in-the-u-s/

Hoeve, M., Dubas, J.S., Gerris, J.R., van der Laan, P.H., & Smeenk, W. (2011). Maternal and paternal parenting styles: unique and combined links to adolescent and early adult delinquency. *Journal of Adolescence 34*(5), 813–827. DOI: 10.1016/j.adolescence.2011.02.004

Hoffman, S.G., Sawyer, A.T., Witt, A.A., & Oh, D. (2010). The effect of mindfulness-based therapy on anxiety and depression: A meta-analytic review. *Journal of Consulting and Clinical Psychology, 78*(2), 169-183. DOI: 10.1037/a0018555

Horvath, A.O., Del Re, A.C., Fluckiger, C., & Symonds, D. (2011). Alliance in individual psychotherapy. *Psychotherapy, 48*(1), 9-16. DOI: 10.1037/a0022186

Huijbers, M.J., Spinhoven, P., van Schaik, D.J.F., Nolen, W.A., & Speckens, A.E.M. (2016). Patients with a preference for medication do equally well in mindfulness-based cognitive therapy for recurrent depression as those preferring mindfulness. *Journal of Affective Disorders, 195*, 32-39. DOI: 10.1016/j.jad.2016.01.041

Hunnicutt Hollenbaugh, K.M., (2011). Treatment compliance in group therapy: Issues and interventions. *Michigan Journal of Counseling: Research, Theory, and Practice, 38*(2), 27-40. Retrieved from https://eric.ed.gov/?id=EJ954601

ICEEFT. (2019). *What is EFT?* Retrieved from https://iceeft.com/what-is-eft/

Institute for Mindfulness-Based Approaches. (2019). *What is MBCT?* Retrieved from https://www.institute-for-mindfulness.org/mbct/what-is-mbct

Johnson, S.M. (2004). *The practice of emotionally focused couple therapy* (2nd ed.). New York, NY: Taylor & Francis.

Johnson, S.M. (2008). *Hold me tight: Seven conversations for a lifetime of love.* New York, NY: Little, Brown and Company.

Johnson, S.M. (2019). Attachment in action – changing the face of 21st century couple therapy. *Current Opinions in Psychology, 25,* 101-104. DOI: 10.1016/j.copsyc.2018.03.007

Johnson, S.R. (2017). *Addressing behavioral health to improve overall health.* Retrieved from https://www.modernhealthcare.com/article/20170527/MAGAZINE/170529956/addressing-behavioral-health-to-improve-all-health

Johnson, S.M., Maddeaux, C., & Blouin, J. (2018). Emotionally focused family therapy for bulimia: Changing attachment patterns. *Psychotherapy, 35*(2), 238-247

Johnson, S.M., & Wittenborn, A.K. (2012). New research findings on emotionally focused therapy: Introduction to special section. *Journal of Marital and Family Therapy, 38,* 18-22. DOI: 10.1111/j.1752-0606.2012.00292.x

Kabat-Zinn, J. (2005). *Wherever you go, there you are: Mindfulness meditation in everyday life.* Boston, MA: Hachette Books.

Kazdin, A.E. (2008). Evidence-based treatment and practice: New opportunities to bridge clinical research and practice, enhance knowledge base and improve patient care. *The American Psychologist, 63,* 146-159, DOI: 10.1037/0003-066X.63.3.146

Keenan, N. (2016). *Electronic devices damage real therapy.* Retrieved from https://nationalpsychologist.com/2016/07/electronic-devices-damage-real-therapy/103340.html

Kerner, I. (2018). *When is it really time for couples therapy?* Retrieved from https://www.cnn.com/2017/07/26/health/couple-therapy-kerner/index.html

Kvarnstrom, W. (2015). *In it together: The importance of the therapeutic alliance.* Retrieved from https://www.bridgestorecovery.com/blog/in-it-together-the-importance-of-the-therapeutic-alliance/

Koolaee, A.K., Lor, S.H., Soleimani, A.A., & Rahmatizadeh, M. (2014). Comparison between family power structure and the quality of parent-child interaction among the delinquent and non-delinquent adolescents. *International Journal of High Risk Behavior and Addiction, 3*(2), online. DOI: 10.5812/ijhrba.13188

Kuusisto, K., Knuuttila, V., & Saarnio, P. (2011). Pre-treatment expectations in clients: Impact on retention and effectiveness in outpatient substance abuse treatment. *Behavioural and Cognitive Psychotherapy, 39*(3), 257-271.

Lacina, D. (2017). *What Hellblade: Senua's Sacrifice gets wrong about mental illness.* Retrieved from https://www.polygon.com/2017/9/15/16316014/hellblade-senuas-sacrifice-mental-illness

Lafrance Robinson, A. L., Dolhanty, J., & Greenberg, L. (2015). Emotion-focused family therapy for eating disorders in children and adolescents. *Clinical Psychology & Psychotherapy, 22*(1), 75-82. DOI: 10.1002/cpp.1861

Larimer, M.E., Palmer, R.S., & Marlatt, G.A. (1999). Relapse prevention: An overview of Marlatt's cognitive-behavioral model. *Alcohol Research & Health, 23*(5), 151-160. Retrieved from https://psycnet.apa.org/record/2000-13161-013

LeBeauf, I., Smaby, M., & Maddux, C. (2009). Adapting counseling skills for multicultural and diverse clients. In G.R. Walz, J.C. Bleuer, & R.K. Yep (Eds.), *Compelling counseling interventions: VISTAS 2009* (pp. 33-42). Alexandria, VA: American Counseling Association.

Lee, M.Y. (2013). Solution-focused brief therapy. *Encyclopedia of Social Work.* DOI: 10.1093/acrefore/9780199975839.013.1039

Levitt, H.M., Pomerville, A., & Surface, F.I. (2016). A qualitative meta-analysis examining clients' experiences of psychotherapy: A new agenda. *Psychology Bulletin, 142*(8), 801-830. DOI: 10.1037/bul0000057

Lewis, B. (2018). *The Gottman Method for couples therapy.* Retrieved from https://www.mindbody7.com/news/2018/1/8/the-gottman-method-for-couples-therapy

Lindstrom, M., Filges, T., & Klint Jorgensen, A.M. (2015). Brief strategic family therapy for young people in treatment for drug use. *Research on Social Work Practice, 25*(1), 61-80, DOI: 10.1177/1049731514530003

Lustbader, R. (2019). *Types and benefits of exposure therapy.* Retrieved from https://www.betterhelp.com/advice/therapy/types-and-benefits-of-exposure-therapy/

Lutz, A., Brefczynski-Lewis, J., Johnstone, T., & Davidson, R.J. (2008). Regulation of the neural circuitry of emotion by compassion meditation: Effects of meditative expertise. *PLoS One, 3*(3). DOI: 10.1371/journal.pone.0001897

Lynch, M.M. (2012). Factors Influencing Successful Psychotherapy Outcomes. Retrieved from https://sophia.stkate.edu/cgi/viewcontent.cgi?article=1057&context=msw_papers

Lytle, M.C., Vaughan, M.D., Rodriguez, E.M., Shmerler, D.L. (2014). Working with LBGT individuals: Incorporating positive psychology into training and practice. *Psychology of Sexual Orientation and Gender Diversity, 1*(4), 335-347. DOI: 10.1037/sgd0000064

MacPherson, H.A., Cheavens, J.S., & Fristad, M.A. (2013). Dialectical behavior therapy for adolescents: Theory, treatment adaptations, and empirical outcomes. *Clinical Child and Family Psychology Review, 16*, 59-80. DOI: 10.1007/s10567-012-0126-7.

Masino Drass, J. (2015). Art therapy for individuals with borderline personality: Using a dialectical behavior therapy framework. *Art Therapy: Journal of the American Art Therapy Association, 32*(4), 168-176. DOI: 10.1080/07421656.2015.1092716

Mayo Clinic. (2019). *Psychotherapy: Overview.* Retrieved from https://www.mayoclinic.org/tests-procedures/psychotherapy/about/pac-20384616

McDonald, T. (2018). *Why the opioid epidemic is a mental health crisis, not a crime wave.* Retrieved from https://www.mentalhealthfirstaid.org/external/2018/04/opioid-epidemic-mental-health-crisis-not-crime-wave/

McHugh, R.K., Whitton, S.W., Peckham, A.D., Welge, J.A., & Otto, M.W. (2013). Patient preference for psychological vs. pharmacological treatment of psychiatric disorders: A meta-analytic review. *Journal of Clinical Psychiatry, 74*(6), 595-602. DOI: 10.4088/JCP.12r07757

McPherson, J. (2012). Does narrative exposure therapy reduce PTSD in survivors of mass violence? *Research on Social Work Practice, 22*(1), 29-42. DOI: 10.1177/104973151141417

Mental Health America. (2018a). *Position Statement 51: Children with emotional disorders in The juvenile justice system.* Retrieved from http://www.mentalhealthamerica.net/positions/juvenile-justice

Mental Health America. (2018b). *The state of mental health in America.* Retrieved from http://www.mentalhealthamerica.net/issues/state-mental-health-america

Mental Health Foundations (2018). Emotion-focused family therapy. Retrieved from http://www.emotionfocusedfamilytherapy.org/efft-the-model/

Meuret, A.E., Twohig, M.P., Rosenfield, D., Hayes, S.C., & Craske, M.G. (2012). Brief acceptance and commitment therapy and exposure for panic disorder: A pilot study. *Cognitive and Behavioral Practice, 19,* 606-618. DOI: 10.1016/j.cbpra.2012.05.004

Meyers, L. (2014). *Connecting with clients.* Retrieved from https://ct.counseling.org/2014/08/connecting-with-clients/

Miller, J. (2016). *Why older adult mental health matters.* Retrieved from http://connections.amhca.org/blogs/joel-miller/2016/02/16/why-older-adult-mental-health-matters

Miller, S.D. (2015). *Becoming a more effective therapist: Three evidence-based clues from research on the field's most effective practitioners.* Retrieved from https://www.scottdmiller.com/becoming-a-more-effective-therapist-three-evidence-based-clues-from-research-on-the-fields-most-effective-practitioners/

Miller, S.D. (2017). *What are the essential qualities of effective therapists?* Retrieved from https://www.psychologytoday.com/us/blog/the-refugee-experience/201703/what-are-the-essential-qualities-effective-therapists

Miller, S.D. (2018). *Psychotherapies most closely held secret: Some practitioners are more effective than others.* Retrieved from https://www.scottdmiller.com/psychotherapys-most-closely-held-secret-some-practitioners-are-more-effective-than-others/

Mindfulurp. (2017). Mindfulness-based relapse prevention. Retrieved from https://www.mindfulrp.com/For-Clinicians.html

Moelbak, R. (2014). *Approaches to couples counseling: The Gottman Method.* Retrieved from http://www.bettertherapy.com/blog/gottman-method/

Morgan-Lopez, A.A., Saavedra, L.M., Hien, D.A., & Fals-Stewart, W. (2011). Estimating statistical power for open enrollment group treatment trials. *Journal of Substance Abuse Treatment, 40,* 3-17. DOI: 10.1016/j.jsa.2010.07.010

National Alliance on Mental Health. (2019a). Juvenile Justice. Retrieved from https://www.nami.org/Learn-More/Mental-Health-Public-Policy/Juvenile-Justice

National Alliance on Mental Illness. (2019b). Mental health by the numbers. Retrieved from https://www.nami.org/learn-more/mental-health-by-the-numbers

National Association of Cognitive-Behavioral Therapists. (n.d.). *What is cognitive-behavioral Therapy (CBT)?* Retrieved from http://www.nacbt.org/whatiscbt-htm/

National Board for Certified Counselors. (2016). *National Board for Certified Counselors (NBCC) policy regarding the provision of distance professional services.* Retrieved http://www.nbcc.org/Assets/Ethics/NBCCPolicyRegardingPracticeofDistanceCounselingboard.pdf

National Center for Mental Health and Juvenile Justice and National Juvenile Justice Network. (2014). *Juvenile justice and mental health and substance abuse disorders fact sheet.* Retrieved from https://act4jj.org/sites/default/files/ckfinder/files/ACT4JJ%20Mental%20Health%20Fact%20Sheet%20August%202014%20FINAL.pdf

National Institute on Drug Abuse. (2018). *Common comorbidities with substance use disorders.* Retrieved from https://www.drugabuse.gov/publications/research-reports/common-comorbidities-substance-use-disorders/why-there-comorbidity-between-substance-use-disorders-mental-illnesses

Najavits, L.M. (2002). *Seeking Safety: A treatment manual for PTSD and substance abuse.* New York, NY: Guilford Press.

Neacsiu, A.D., Ward-Ciesielski, E.F., & Linehan, M.M. (2012). Emerging approaches to counseling intervention: Dialectical behavior therapy. *The Counseling Psychologist, 40*(7), 1003-1032. DOI: 10.1177/0011000011421023

Newman, K. (2017). *A look into older adults' state of mind.* Retrieved from https://www.usnews.com/news/best-states/articles/2017-10-11/older-adults-struggle-to-get-adequate-mental-health-care

Nichols, H. (2018). *The top 10 mental health apps.* Retrieved from https://www.medicalnewstoday.com/articles/320557.php

Nissen, P. (2011). *Theory and evidence-based intervention: Practice-based evidence – integrating positive psychology into a clinical psychological assessment and intervention model and how to measure outcome. Psychology Research, 1*(2), 91-105. Retrieved from https://files.eric.ed.gov/fulltext/ED535718.pdf

Norcross, J.C., & Wampold, B.E. (2011). Evidence-based therapy relationships: Research conclusions and clinical practices. *Psychotherapy, 48*(1), 98-102. DOI: 10.1037/a0022161

Oberlander, J. (2010). Long time coming: Why health reform finally passed. *Health Affairs, 29*(6). DOI: 10.1377/hlthaff.2010.0447

Office of Juvenile Justice and Delinquency Prevention. (2017). *Intersection between mental health and the juvenile justice system.* Retrieved from https://www.ojjdp.gov/mpg/litreviews/Intersection-Mental-Health-Juvenile-Justice.pdf

Online Counseling Programs. (2017). *10 multicultural factors to consider in counseling.* Retrieved from https://onlinecounselingprograms.com/blog/multicultural-counseling-model/

Pachankis, D. (2016). *Evidenced-based treatments for mental health among LGB clients.* Retrieved from https://www.div12.org/evidence-based-treatments-for-mental-health-among-lgb-clients/

Patitz, B.J., Anderson, M.L., & Navajits, L.M. (2015). An outcome study of seeking safety with rural community-based women. *Journal of Rural Mental Health, 39*(1), 54-58. DOI: 10.1037/rmh0000015

Patterson, C.L., Uhlin, B., & Anderson, T. (2008). Clients' pretreatment counseling expectations as predictors of the working alliance. *Journal of Counseling Psychology, 55*(4), 528-534, DOI: 10.1037/a0013289

PhysicianAssistantEDU. (2019). *How to become a PA specialized in psychiatry/mental health.* Retrieved from https://www.physicianassistantedu.org/psychiatry-mental-health/

Pistorello, J., Fruzzetti, A.E., MacLane, C., Gallop, R., & Iverson, K. (2012). Dialectical behavior therapy (DBT) applied to college students: A randomized clinical trial. *Journal of Consulting and Clinical Psychology, 80*(6), 982-994. DOI: 10.1037/a0029096

Ponton, L. (2018). *Characteristics of effective counseling.* Retrieved from https://psychcentral.com/lib/characteristics-of-effective-counseling/

Psychology Today. (2019). *The Gottman Method.* Retrieved from https://www.psychologytoday.com/us/therapy-types/the-gottman-method

Ratts, M.J., Singh, A.A., Nassar-McMillan, S., Butler, S.K., & McCullough, J.R. (2015). *Multicultural and Social Justice Counseling Competencies.* Retrieved from https://www.counseling.org/docs/default-source/competencies/multicultural-and-social-justice-counseling-competencies.pdf?sfvrsn=8573422c_20

Ratts, M.J., Singh, A.A., Butler, S.K., Nassar-McMillan, S., and McCullough, J.R. (2016). Multicultural and social justice counseling: Practical applications in counseling. *Counseling Today.* Retrieved from https://ct.counseling.org/2016/01/multicultural-and-social-justice-counseling-competencies-practical-applications-in-counseling/

Rauch, J. (2016). *Here's what makes a good therapist: 17 signs to look for.* Retrieved from https://www.talkspace.com/blog/heres-makes-good-therapist-17-signs-look/

Reardon, C. (2015). More than toys – gamer affirmative therapy. *Social Work Today*, 15(3), 10. Retrieved from https://www.socialworktoday.com/archive/051815p10.shtml

Richards, D. (2018). *Tackling the mental health epidemic with telehealth.* Retrieved from https://www.healthitoutcomes.com/doc/tackling-the-mental-health-epidemic-with-telehealth-0001

Ritchie, H. & Roser, M. (2018). Mental Health. *Our World in Data.* Retrieved from https://ourworldindata.org/mental-health

Rizvi, S.L. (2011). Treatment failure in dialectical behavior therapy. *Cognitive and Behavioral Practice, 18*(3), 403-412. DOI: 10.1016/j.cbpra.2010.05.003

Robbins, M.S., & Szapocznik, J. (2000). *Brief strategic family therapy.* Juvenile Justice Bulletin, U.S. Department of Justice. Retrieved from https://www.ncjrs.gov/pdffiles1/ojjdp/179285.pdf

Robin, A.L., Siegel, P.T., Moye, A.W., Gilroy, M., Baker Dennis, A., & Sikand, A. (1999). A controlled comparison of family versus individual therapy for adolescents with anorexia nervosa. *Journal of the American Academy of Child and Adolescent Psychiatry, 38*(12), 1482-1480. DOI: 10.1097/00004583-199912000-00008

Roessel, M.H. (2018). *Working with indigenous/Native American patients.* Retrieved from https://www.psychiatry.org/psychiatrists/cultural-competency/treating-diverse-patient-populations/working-with-native-american-patients

Sackett, D. L., Straus, S. E., Richardson, W. S., Rosenberg, W., & Haynes, R. B. (2000). *Evidence based medicine: How to practice and teach EBM* (2$^{nd}$ ed.). London, UK: Churchill Livingstone.

Schaeffer, C.M., Bruns, E., Weist, M., Hoover Stephan, S., Goldstein, J., & Simpson, Y. (2005). overcoming challenges to using evidence-based interventions in schools. *Journal of Youth and Adolescence, 34*(1), 15-22.

Schare, M.L., & Wyatt, K.P. (2013). On the evolving nature of exposure therapy. *Behavior Modification, 37*(2), 243-256. DOI: 10.1177/0145445513477421

Selva, J. (2018). What is evidence-based therapy: 3 EBT interventions. Retrieved from https://positivepsychologyprogram.com/evidence-based-therapy/

Sexton, T., & Turner, C.W. (2011). The effectiveness of functional family therapy for youth with behavioral problems in a community practice setting. *Couple and Family Psychology: Research and Practice, 1*(S), 3-15. DOI: 10.1037/2160-4096.1.S/3

Simon, G. (2016). *Effective therapist qualities and CBT.* Retrieved from https://counsellingresource.com/features/2016/10/03/effective-therapist-qualities/

Sipe, W.E., & Eisendrath, S.J. (2012). Mindfulness-based cognitive therapy: Theory and practice. *Canadian Journal of Psychiatry, 57*(2), 63-69. DOI: 10.1177/070674371205700202

Strahan, E. J., Stillar, A., Files, N., Nash, P., Scarborough, J., Connors, L., ... & Lafrance, A. (2017). Increasing parental self-efficacy with Emotion-Focused Family Therapy for eating disorders: a process model. *Person-*

*Centered & Experiential Psychotherapies, 16*(3), 256-269. DOI: 10.1080/14770757.2017.1330703

Stuntzner, S. & Hartley, M.T. (2014). *Disability and the counseling relationship: What counselors need to know.* Retrieved from https://www.counseling.org/docs/default-source/vistas/article_09.pdf?sfvrsn=157ccf7c_12

Swales, M.A. (2009). Dialectical behavior therapy: Description, research, and future directions. *International Journal of Behavioral Consultation and Therapy, 5*(2), 164-177. Retrieved from https://files.eric.ed.gov/fulltext/EJ880555.pdf

Swift, J.K., Callahan, J.L., & Levine, J.C. (2009). Using clinically significant change to identify premature termination. *Psychotherapy: Theory, Research, Practice, Training, 46,* 328-335. DOI: 10.1037/a0017003

Swift, J.K., & Greenberg, R.P. (2012). Premature discontinuation in adult psychotherapy: A meta-analysis. *Journal of Consulting and Clinical Psychology, 80*(4), 547-559. DOI: 10.1037/a0028226

Teasdale, J.D., Segal, Z.V., & Williams, J.M.G. (1995). How does cognitive therapy prevent depressive relapse and why should attentional control (mindfulness) training help? *Behaviour Research and Therapy, 33*(1), 25-39. DOI: 10.1016/0005-7967(94)E0011-7

The Gottman Institute. (2019). *The Gottman Method.* Retrieved from https://www.gottman.com/about/the-gottman-method/

Tomikawa, Y. (2017). *The 6 benefits and limitations of remote video therapy.* Retrieved from https://www.zencare.co/blog/posts/the-6-benefits-and-limitations-of-remote-video-therapy

Torous, J., Luo, J., & Chan, S. (2018). Mental health apps: What to tell patients. *Current Psychiatry, 17*(3), 21-25. Retrieved from https://www.digitalpsych.org/uploads/3/0/2/2/30224051/0318cp_torous_to_author.pdf

Treatment Innovations. (2016). Seeking Safety. Retrieved from https://www.treatment-innovations.org/ss-description.html

Tucci, V. & Moukaddam, N. (2017). We are the hollow men: The worldwide epidemic of mental illness, psychiatric and behavioral emergencies, and its impact on patients and providers. *Journal of Emergencies, Trauma, and Shock,* (10)1, 4-6. DOI: 10.4103/0974-2700.199517

USCD Center for Mindfulness. (2019a). MBRP: Mindfulness-based relapse prevention. Retrieved from http://mbpti.org/programs/mbrp/mbrp-intensive/

UCSD Center for Mindfulness. (2019b). MCBT Overview. Retrieved from http://mbpti.org/programs/mbct-overview/

Vandervord Nixon, R.D., Sterk, J., & Pearce, A. (2012). A randomized trial of cognitive behaviour therapy and cognitive therapy for children with posttraumatic stress disorder following single-incident trauma. *Journal of Abnormal Child Psychology, 40,* 327-337. DOI: 10.1007/s10802-011-9566-7

Villa, L. (n.d.). *Treating substance abuse & co-occurring mental illness.* Retrieved from https://www.projectknow.com/co-occurring-disorders/

Vitelli, R. (2014). *Are there benefits in playing video games?* Retrieved from https://www.psychologytoday.com/us/blog/media-spotlight/201402/are-there-benefits-in-playing-video-games

Wampold, B.E. (2011). *Qualities and actions of effective therapists.* Retrieved from https://www.apa.org/education/ce/effective-therapists.pdf

Wake Forest University. (n.d.). How family counselors teach communication skills. Retrieved from https://counseling.online.wfu.edu/blog/how-family-counselors-teach-communication-skills/

Wiebe, S.A. & Johnson, S.M. (2016). A review of the research in emotionally focused therapy for couples. *Family Process, 55*(3), 390-407. DOI: 10.1111/famp.12229

Wierzbicki, M., & Pekarik, G. (1993). A meta-analysis of psychotherapy dropout. *Professional Psychology: Research and Practice, 24*(2), 190-195. DOI: 10.1037/0728.24.2.190

Witkiewitz, K., & Bowen, S. (2010). Depression, craving, and substance use following a randomized trial of mindfulness-based relapse prevention. *Journal of Counseling and Clinical Psychology, 78*(3), 362-374. DOI: 10.1037/a0019172

Wong, D.F.K., Kwok, S.Y.C.L., Tsang Low, Y., Wei Man, K., & Ip, P.S.Y. (2018). Evaluating effectiveness of cognitive-behavior therapy for Hong Kong adolescents with anxiety problems. *Research on Social Work Practice, 28*(5), 585-594. DOI: 10.1177/1049731516658351

World Health Organization. (2017). *Mental health of older adults.* Retrieved from https://www.who.int/news-room/fact-sheets/detail/mental-health-of-older-adults

World Health Organization. (2018). *Mental disorders.* Retrieved from https://www.who.int/news-room/fact-sheets/detail/mental-disorders

Zaboski, B.A., Schrack, A.P., Joyce-Beaulieu, D., & MacInnes, J.W. (2017). Broadening our understanding of evidence-based practice: Effective and discredited interventions. *Contemporary School Psychology, 21*(3), 287-297. DOI: 10.1007/s40688-017-0131-4

# About the Authors

**Nicholas D. Young, PhD, EdD**

Dr. Nicholas D. Young has worked in diverse educational roles for more than 30 years, serving as a teacher, counselor, principal, special education director, graduate professor, graduate program director, graduate dean, and longtime psychologist and superintendent of schools. He was named the Massachusetts Superintendent of the Year; and he completed a distinguished Fulbright program focused on the Japanese educational system through the collegiate level. Dr. Young is the recipient of numerous other honors and recognitions including the General Douglas MacArthur Award for distinguished civilian and military leadership and the Vice Admiral John T. Hayward Award for exemplary scholarship. He holds several graduate degrees including a PhD in educational administration and an EdD in educational psychology.

Dr. Young has served in the U.S. Army and U.S. Army Reserves combined for over 34 years; and he graduated with distinction from the U.S. Air War College, the U.S. Army War College, and the U.S. Navy War College. After completing a series of senior leadership assignments in the U.S. Army Reserves as the commanding officer of the 287th Medical Company (DS), the 405th Area Support Company (DS), the 405th Combat Support Hospital, and the 399th Combat Support Hospital, he transitioned to his current military position as a faculty instructor at the U.S. Army War College in Carlisle, PA. He currently holds the rank of Colonel.

Dr. Young is also a regular presenter at state, national, and international conferences; and he has written many books, book chapters, and/or articles on various topics in education, counseling, and psychology. Some of his most recent books include *Masculinity in the Making: Managing the Transition to Manhood* (in-press); *The Burden of Being a Boy: Bolstering Educational and Emotional Well-Being in Young Males* (in-press); *The Special Education Toolbox: Supporting Exceptional Teachers, Students, and Families* (2019); *Sounding the Alarm in the Schoolhouse: Safety, Security and Student Well-Being* (2019); *Creating Compassionate Classrooms: Understanding the*

*Continuum of Disabilities and Effective Educational Interventions* (2019); *Acceptance, Understanding, and the Moral Imperative of Promoting Social Justice Education in the Schoolhouse* (2019); *Empathic Teaching: Promoting Social Justice in the Contemporary Classroom* (2019); *Educating the Experienced: Challenges and Best Practices in Adult Learning* (2019); *Securing the Schoolyard: Protocols that Promote Safety and Positive Student Behaviors* (2018); *The Soul of the Schoolhouse: Cultivating Student Engagement* (2018); *Embracing and Educating the Autistic Child: Valuing Those Who Color Outside the Lines* (2018); *From Cradle to Classroom: A Guide to Special Education for Young Children* (2018); *Captivating Classrooms: Educational Strategies to Enhance Student Engagement* (2018); *Potency of the Principalship: Action-Oriented Leadership at the Heart of School Improvement* (2018); *Soothing the Soul: Pursuing a Life of Abundance Through a Practice of Gratitude* (2018); *Dog Tags to Diploma: Understanding and Addressing the Educational Needs of Veterans, Servicemembers, and their Families* (2018); *Turbulent Times: Confronting Challenges in Emerging Adulthood* (2018); *Guardians of the Next Generation: Igniting the Passion for Quality Teaching* (2018); *Achieving Results: Maximizing Success in the Schoolhouse* (2018); *From Head to Heart: High Quality Teaching Practices in the Spotlight* (2018); *Stars in the Schoolhouse: Teaching Practices and Approaches that Make a Difference* (2018); *Making the Grade: Promoting Positive Outcomes for Students with Learning Disabilities* (2018); *Paving the Pathway for Educational Success: Effective Classroom Interventions for Students with Learning Disabilities* (2018); *Wrestling with Writing: Effective Strategies for Struggling Students* (2018); *Floundering to Fluent: Reaching and Teaching the Struggling Student* (2018); *Emotions and Education: Promoting Positive Mental Health in Students with Learning* (2018); *From Lecture Hall to Laptop: Opportunities, Challenges, and the Continuing Evolution of Virtual Learning in Higher Education* (2017); *The Power of the Professoriate: Demands, Challenges, and Opportunities in $21^{st}$ Century Higher Education* (2017); *To Campus with Confidence: Supporting a Successful Transition to College for Students with Learning Disabilities* (2017); *Educational Entrepreneurship: Promoting Public-Private Partnerships for the 21st Century* (2015); *Beyond the Bedtime Story: Promoting Reading Development during the Middle School Years* (2015); *Betwixt and Between: Understanding and Meeting the Social and Emotional Developmental Needs of Students During the Middle School Transition Years* (2014); *Learning Style Perspectives: Impact Upon the Classroom* (3rd ed., 2014); and *Collapsing Educational Boundaries from Preschool to PhD: Building Bridges Across the Educational Spectrum* (2013); *Transforming Special Education Practices: A Primer for School Administrators and Policy Makers* (2012); and *Powerful Partners in Student Success: Schools, Families and Communities* (2012). He also co-authored several children's books to include the popular series *I am Full of Possibilities*. Dr. Young may be contacted directly at nyoung1191@aol.com.

## Melissa A. Mumby, EdD

Dr. Mumby has worked in various levels of K-12 education for over a decade. She began her career as a high school English and drama teacher, and then transitioned into a role as a special educator, working with both middle and high school students. From there she became a special education coordinator for grades K-5, and eventually the special education director for grades K-12 at a local charter school. She is currently an educational team leader in an urban public school district in Massachusetts. Dr. Mumby holds an undergraduate degree in English Literature from the University of Massachusetts, Amherst, as well as an MEd and EdD. from American International College, both in education. Her dissertation, "Is there an app for that? Teachers' perceptions of the impact of digital tools on literacy in the secondary classroom" focused on the ways in which technology can increase learning outcomes for struggling learners. She has written book chapters on strategies for helping underperforming students find success in the classroom and she is a primary author on *The Special Education Toolbox: Supporting Exceptional Teachers, Students, and Families* (2019); *Educating the Experienced: Challenges and Best Practices in Adult Learning* (2019); *Embracing and Educating the Autistic Child: Valuing Those Who Color Outside the Lines* (2018). Dr. Mumby can be reached at mumbym@springfieldpublicschools.com.

## Jennifer A. Smolinski, J.D.

Attorney Jennifer Smolinski has worked in education for more than three years. Her role within higher education includes the creation of, and coordinator for, the Center for Accessibility Services and Academic Accommodations at American International College located in Springfield, Massachusetts. She has also taught criminal justice and legal research and writing classes within the field of higher education. Prior to her work at the collegiate level, Attorney Smolinski worked as a solo-practitioner conducting education and disability advocacy.

Attorney Smolinski received a Bachelor of Arts in Anthropology and Bachelor of Arts in Sociology from the University of Connecticut, a master's in psychology and Counseling as well as a master's of Higher Education Student Affairs from Salem State University and her law degree from Massachusetts School of Law. She is currently an EdD in Educational Leadership and Supervision candidate at American International College, where she is focusing her research on special education and laws to protect students with disabilities in the classroom.

Attorney Smolinski has become a regular presenter educating the faculty, staff and students at institutes of higher education on disabilities and accommodations at the collegiate level and has presented to local high school special education departments on the transition to college under the Americans with Disabilities Act. She has co-authored *Securing the Schoolyard: Protocols that Promote Safety and Positive Student Behaviors* (2018); *Sounding the Alarm in the Schoolhouse: Safety, Security and Student Well-Being* (2018); *Captivating Classrooms: Educational Strategies to Enhance Student Engagement* (2018); *Guardian of the Next Generation: Igniting the Passion for Quality Teaching* (2018); and *Making the Grade: Promoting Positive Outcomes for Students with Learning Disabilities* (2018). She can be reached at Jennifer.Smolinski@aic.edu.

www.ingramcontent.com/pod-product-compliance
Lightning Source LLC
Chambersburg PA
CBHW061843300426
44115CB00013B/2484